APPLAUSE

Oklahoma's Best Performing Recipes

Oklahoma City Orchestra League, Inc.

Since its organization in 1948, the mission of the Oklahoma City Orchestra League, Inc. has been to improve the quality of life in our community through effective volunteerism. Over the years, hundreds of men and women have contributed their talent, their time and their personal resources to provide Oklahoma City with a fine orchestra, innovative projects in the public schools and libraries as well as scholarship opportunities for young people. The Orchestra League continues to work tirelessly for the enrichment of our community. Proceeds from **Applause** will be returned to the community to expand upon these many cultural programs.

*Additional copies of **Applause** may be obtained by writing or calling:*

APPLAUSE
The Oklahoma City Orchestra League, Inc.
Fifty Penn Place Suite R325
Oklahoma City, OK 73118
(405) 84–BRAVA

First Edition, First Printing 10,000 copies

Copyright 1995
The Oklahoma City Orchestra League, Inc.
Oklahoma City, Oklahoma

ISBN 0–9643907–0–1
Library of Congress Card Catalog Number 95-67491

Printed in the United States of America
TOOF COOKBOOK DIVISION

STARR★TOOF

670 South Cooper Street
Memphis, TN 38104

CONTENTS

Meet the Artist

Virginia Vann whose collage and design appears on the cover of **Applause** has a distinctive style based upon spontaneity and color. Her recent work includes acrylics and abstract design, as well as costume jewelry and clay pottery. Her line drawings illustrate her keen ability to capture the spirit of the moment.

Vann's work has won numerous awards and may be found in private collections from Florida to California. She resides in Oklahoma City with her husband, Bob.

In Applause, we provide you with a short cut to your food selections. Look for:

 Recipes with your heart in mind!

 Simple dishes when time is short.

 Food memories from on the road.

 Favorites from the Festivals

 International specialties

 You're preparing for a crowd? Try these.

WELCOME

The Oklahoma City Orchestra League, Inc. is proud to present **APPLAUSE** . . . Oklahoma's Best Performing Recipes.

This collection of 400 well–tested and tasted recipes reflects the cultural heritage, music, art and wonderful food which is truly Oklahoma.

APPLAUSE goes beyond just presenting the "best performing" recipes for your kitchen. Through good food, this book show-cases the many festivals, the museums, the music and many other "best kept" secrets whose recipes for achievement have successfully enriched the lives of all of us.

Whether it's a recipe from Celeste Holm who played "Ado Annie" in the original cast of the musical, **Oklahoma**, or a deli-cious kolache so popular at the annual Czech Festival, **APPLAUSE** presents a kaleidoscope of a state diverse in ethnic heritage, cultural presence and courageous spirit. Oklahomans are ready to greet the 21st Century while keeping alive the finest family traditions brought here over a hundred years ago by covered wagons and "surreys with the fringe on the top".

When you open these pages, you will readily see why Oklahoma is a state we wish to applaud and happily share with you.

APPETIZERS

RODGERS and HAMMERSTEIN'S OKLAHOMA!

APPETIZERS

Cold Appetizers
Caponata,9
Cashew Chicken Balls,16
Caviar Spread,19
Chicken Liver Paté, 17
Curry Chicken Spread,17
Gala Cheese Ball,15
Greek Cheese,14
Ham Squares,19
Okie Caviar,12
Olive and Caper Tapenade,11
Party Cheese Log,15
Rosemary Walnuts, 16
Salmon Mousse,20
Shrimp Spread,20
Stuffed Tortillas,13
Yogurt Dip,13

Hot Appetizers
Blackeyed Pea Dip,12
Bleu Crab Fondue,22
Chilmark Chips,11
Crab Stuffed Mushroom Caps,21

Grilled Lemon Chicken Wings,18
Hot Lobster Dip,21
Nutty Baked Camembert,14
Red Pepper Hors d'Oeuvres,10
Roasted Garlic,9
Sausage Pastry Turnovers,18
Spicy Cocktail Beef,23
Spinach Stuffed Mushrooms,10
Swiss Ryes,15

BEVERAGES
Brandy Ice for a Crowd,28
Champagne Punch,24
Citrus Bourbon Slush,28
Cranberry Punch,25
Frozen Margaritas,27
Frozen Banana Punch,25
Hot Spiced Cider,26
Orange Smoothie,26
Rum Mint Cooler,27
Southern Iced Coffee Punch,25
Strawberry Lemonade Punch,24
Tropical Ice,26

OKLAHOMA!

The Rogers and Hammerstein musical, **Oklahoma!**, which opened March 31, 1943, changed the direction of musical theater forever. Combining for the first time drama, musical theatre and ballet, **Oklahoma!** still captures the hearts of all who enter a quiet theater to see a woman churning butter and hear a lone cowboy off-stage singing, "Oh What A Beautiful Morning." This enchanting melody has been adopted as the theme song for a network morning television show. And, as might be expected, the exciting title song became the official State Song for Oklahoma.

Caponata

A Bartlesville favorite!

Barbara Bonifazi Williams — 48 servings

2 medium eggplants
2 large onions, chopped
½ cup olive oil
1 ½ cups celery, sliced
2 red bell peppers, chopped
2 green bell peppers, chopped
2 garlic cloves, minced
2 ½ pounds tomatoes, peeled and seeded
⅓ cup red wine vinegar
2 tablespoons salt
¼ cup fresh basil, chopped
3 tablespoons tomato paste
½ cup parsley, chopped
1 teaspoon freshly ground pepper
¾ cup green olives, sliced

- Cut unpeeled eggplant into 1-inch cubes. Heat olive oil in 5 or 6-quart Dutch oven.
- Sauté eggplant and onion for five minutes. Add remaining ingredients. Stir gently, but thoroughly.
- Simmer, covered, for 30 minutes. Remove lid and simmer 10 minutes more.
- Serve at room temperature with slices of Italian bread.

Roasted Garlic

Dorothy Dinsmoor — 2 servings

1 large complete bulb of garlic
extra virgin olive oil
salt and pepper to taste

- Preheat oven to 275 degrees.
- Slice off the top of the bulb of garlic, partially removing the outer skin. Leave the cloves attached. Brush the top with olive oil and sprinkle with salt and pepper. Place in a ceramic baking dish or garlic roaster. Cover tightly and bake for one hour. Baste again with olive oil and bake another hour.
- Serve warm for guests to spread on French bread or crackers.

Hint: After this is baked, the garlic softens and has a mellow, slightly sweet flavor.

9

Red Pepper Hors D'Oeuvres

A delicious Tulsa recipe!

Cynthia Williams Stewart   24 servings

1 petit pain (small diameter French bread)
2 tablespoons olive oil
low-fat ricotta cheese
1 jar (7 ounce) roasted red peppers

> Calories per serving: 24
> Saturated Fat 1 g
> Cholesterol 3 mg
> Total Fat 2 g (69% of Calories)
> Sodium 11 mg

- Slice petit pain into ½-inch rounds.
- Brush each bread round with olive oil and spread with ricotta cheese. Top with roasted red peppers.
- Broil on cookie sheet until cheese softens and edges of bread turn light brown.

Variation: Prepare your own peppers by julienne-cutting 2 large red bell peppers. Toss with ½ cup Lawry's Herb and Garlic Marinade. Bake at 325 degrees until tender, stirring occasionally, approximately 25 minutes.

Spinach Stuffed Mushrooms

Diane Henderson   30 mushrooms

1 package (10 ounce) frozen chopped spinach
½ cup sour cream
¼ cup tomato sauce
1 dash red wine vinegar
1 cup Parmesan cheese, grated
30 fresh mushrooms, stems removed
4 tablespoons butter, melted

- Preheat oven to 350 degrees.
- Cook spinach according to package directions and drain well. Add remaining ingredients. Mix well.
- Dip mushrooms in butter and fill with spinach mixture. Place in baking dish.
- Bake 15 minutes or until bubbly.

Hint: Stuff larger mushrooms and use as an accompaniment for beef.

Olive and Caper Tapenade

Laura Lewis — 48 servings

1 ½ cups cured olives, pitted
1 tablespoon capers
1 can (2 ounce) anchovy filets
1 to 2 tablespoons extra virgin olive oil
1 tablespoon lemon juice
1 tablespoon cognac

- Pound the olives, capers and anchovies in a mortar to form a paste. Dribble in the oil, stirring continually.
- Mix in lemon juice and cognac. Let stand at room temperature 1 hour before serving with celery stalks and small rounds of grilled bread.

Chilmark Chips

Mrs. Guy Fraser Harrison — 6 servings

6 Idaho potatoes, scrubbed, unpeeled
salt
dill seed

Calories per serving: 225
Saturated Fat 0 g
Cholesterol 0 mg
Total Fat 0 g (0% of Calories)
Sodium 800 mg

- Preheat oven to 500 degrees.
- Slice potatoes very thin and place on a nonstick cookie sheet. Do not overlap slices.
- Sprinkle with salt and dill seed. Place in oven and immediately lower temperature to 475 degrees. Bake 12 minutes. Potatoes will be puffed and brown. Depending on moisture content of potatoes, time may vary from 10 to 14 minutes.
- Serve immediately in heated container. Do not cover.

Guy Fraser Harrison was the conductor of the Oklahoma City Symphony from 1951 to 1975. The weekly radio broadcasts, featuring new American compositions, launched many new composers whose works today may be heard in concert halls around the world. Several times, Dr. Harrison received the A.S.C.A.P. Award for promoting works by living, American composers.

Okie Caviar

Ina Lou Marquiss   7 cups

1 can pinto beans with jalapeños,
drained
1 can blackeyed peas with
jalapeños, drained
1 can white hominy, drained
2 medium tomatoes, chopped
4 green onions, chopped
½ cup parsley, chopped
2 garlic cloves, crushed
1 green pepper, chopped
½ cup onion, chopped
1 cup Italian salad dressing
picante sauce (optional)

- Combine all ingredients. Mix well. Cover and refrigerate, to marinate, for at least two hours.
- Drain and serve with fresh tortilla chips. Fat free salad dressing may be used.

Blackeyed Pea Dip

Dixie Jensen   6 to 8 servings

¼ cup butter
1 medium onion, chopped
1 package (10 ounce) Cheddar
cheese
2 jars (5 ounce) Old English cheese
1 can blackeyed peas
1 can (4 ounce) chopped green
chiles
2 cans (4 ounce) ripe olives,
chopped
garlic salt and black pepper to
taste

- Sauté onion in butter in top of double boiler. Add cheeses. Heat until cheese melts, stirring occasionally.
- Add remaining ingredients; mix well.

Hint: You may control the amount of "heat" in this dip by using mild, medium or hot chiles. It's your choice!

Stuffed Tortillas

Jeanne Byler   40 servings

2 packages (8 ounce) cream cheese, softened
1 can (4 ounce) chopped green chiles
1 can (4 ounce) ripe olives, chopped
8 green onions, chopped (including tops)
¼ teaspoon Nature's Seasoning
⅛ teaspoon garlic powder
6 flour tortillas (soft)
picante sauce

- Mix cream cheese with all ingredients. Spread mixture on soft flour tortillas. Roll up and refrigerate.
- Before serving, slice ¼ inch thick.
- Serve with toothpicks for dipping in picante sauce.

Hint: You may use "light" cream cheese.

Yogurt Dip

Lu Garrison   40 servings

3 cups plain yogurt (nonfat optional)
3 jars (8 ounce) medium thick and chunky salsa
2 small garlic cloves, peeled and crushed
4 green onions, chopped

- Blend all ingredients well; chill. Serve with chips or freshly prepared vegetables.

Calories per serving: 15
Saturated Fat 0 g
Cholesterol 0 mg
Total Fat 0 g (0% of Calories)
Sodium 80 mg

Greek Cheese

Susan Hatcher · 12 servings

1 garlic clove, crushed
1 package (8 ounce) cream cheese, softened
¼ cup sour cream
1 package (2 ounce) feta cheese, crumbled
1 tablespoon fresh lemon juice
¼ cup parsley, chopped
¼ cup green onions, chopped
1 tablespoon fresh mint, chopped
2 teaspoons fresh oregano, chopped
pinch each of nutmeg and cinnamon
salt as needed

- Bring all ingredients to room temperature and combine in food processor. Refrigerate and allow time for the flavors to blend. Spread on crackers or hot bread.

Sand Springs' Susan Hatcher shares her favorite appetizer from the Oklahoma Herbal Festival Cookbook.

Nutty Baked Camembert

Perfect after theater treat with champagne.

Kelly Shoemaker · 4 servings

¼ cup pecan or walnut halves
1 loaf (4 ½ ounce) Camembert cheese
1 egg
apple or pear slices
brioche or raisin pumpernickel bread

- Preheat oven to 350 degrees.
- Toast nuts at 350 degrees for 12 to 15 minutes, until lightly browned. Cool them and finely chop.
- Beat the egg in a shallow dish and turn the cheese in it to coat well. Then cover with pecans, pressing them in.
- Bake at 350 degrees for 10 minutes until hot and slightly runny.
- Serve at once with apple or pear slices and lightly toasted rich bread.

Swiss Ryes

Maurine Gatewood
3 dozen

1 cup Swiss cheese, finely grated
¼ cup bacon, cooked and crumbled
1 can (4 ½ ounce) ripe olives, chopped
¼ cup green onions, minced
1 teaspoon Worcestershire sauce
¼ cup mayonnaise
party rye bread

- Preheat oven to 375 degrees.
- Mix all ingredients together and spread on party rye or pumpernickel.
- Bake 15 minutes or until browned.

Party Cheese Log

A winner at the Okmulgee Pecan Festival

Mable L. Osborne
20 servings

2 packages (8 ounce) cream cheese, softened
1 package (8 ounce) sharp Cheddar cheese, shredded
1 tablespoon pimiento, chopped
1 tablespoon green pepper, finely chopped
2 tablespoons Worcestershire sauce
1 tablespoon onion, finely chopped
dash hot sauce
½ cup pecans, chopped

- Blend cheeses in a medium bowl. Add remaining ingredients except pecans. Mix well. Chill. Shape into a log. Roll in chopped nuts. Serve with crackers.

Gala Cheese Ball

Verna Miller
40 servings

1 package (8 ounce) sharp Cheddar cheese
1 package (16 ounce) mild Cheddar or longhorn cheese
1 package (8 ounce) cream cheese
4 tablespoons bleu cheese or Roquefort salad dressing
2 tablespoons onion, diced
½ teaspoon Worcestershire sauce
fresh parsley, chopped

- Mix onion with cream cheese in a food processor. Add other ingredients except parsley and process until smooth.
- Shape into a ball and gently roll in parsley. Refrigerate overnight, tightly wrapped, to blend flavors. Serve with a spreader and an assortment of crackers.

Hint: Makes a nice gift! Just wrap in clear plastic and add an appropriate bow.

15

Rosemary Walnuts

Dennis Shrock   2 cups

2 cups shelled walnut halves
2 tablespoons butter, melted
2 teaspoons dried rosemary,
crumbled
½ teaspoon salt
¼ teaspoon cayenne pepper

- Preheat oven to 350 degrees.
- Place walnuts in a shallow baking pan, spreading them in a single layer. Mix the remaining ingredients and pour over the walnuts, stirring to coat the nuts.
- Roast about 10 minutes or until lightly browned. Watch nuts carefully the final two minutes of roasting to avoid overbrowning.

Mr. Shrock conducts the Canterbury Choral Society which is the official chorus of the Philharmonic Orchestra. Outstanding voices from all over central Oklahoma audition to be part of this excellent group.

Cashew Chicken Balls

Jill Mizel   20 balls

½ cup cooked chicken, diced
½ onion
½ cup sharp Cheddar cheese,
shredded
salt to taste
¼ teaspoon pepper
2 tablespoons dry sherry
½ cup cashews, finely chopped

- Place onion in food processor and finely chop. Add chicken and process briefly until coarsely chopped. Do not purée.
- Combine all ingredients, except the cashews, in a large mixing bowl. Form into 20 balls. Roll in the cashews. Chill well before serving. Do not freeze.

Curry Chicken Spread

Carol David   8 servings

1 package (8 ounce) cream cheese,
softened
½ cup mayonnaise
2 teaspoons lemon juice
½ teaspoon salt
¼ teaspoon curry powder
⅛ teaspoon pepper
2 cups cooked chicken, finely
minced
½ cup mango chutney
¼ cup green onions, chopped

- Blend first 7 ingredients and spread in a serving dish. Layer the mango chutney over the top. Garnish with chopped green onions. Serve with crackers.

Chicken Liver Paté

John Bennett   40 servings

2 pounds chicken livers
2 tablespoons butter
2 tablespoons vegetable oil
1 medium onion, sliced
2 garlic cloves
1 unpeeled apple, cored and
chopped
1 teaspoon tarragon vinegar
½ cup dry sherry
4 eggs, hard cooked
salt, pepper, Tabasco, lemon juice
to taste.

- Sauté chicken livers in butter and oil over medium heat. Add onion, garlic, apple, vinegar and sherry. Cook together until onions are translucent but not brown and the apple is soft. Allow to cool.

- Blend cooked ingredients, eggs and sherry in food processor or blender. Add salt, pepper, Tabasco and lemon juice to taste and blend until desired consistency. Use more sherry if needed.

- Paté will keep well for a week or 10 days in the refrigerator.

John Bennett, a favorite Oklahoma chef at "The Cellar", featured this recipe in one of his superb cooking classes. A cocktail buffet stand-out!

Grilled Lemon Buttered Chicken Wings

Martha Findeiss   16 servings.

LEMON BUTTER SAUCE
juice of 6 large lemons
1 cup butter, melted
1 tablespoon salt
1 tablespoon black pepper
1 tablespoon sugar
¼ teaspoon dry mustard
3 tablespoons Worcestershire sauce
2 tablespoons dried rosemary, crushed, (optional)
16 chicken wings

- Wisk sauce ingredients. Set aside.
- Remove the wing tips from chicken wings, then divide each piece into 2 segments. Wash and dry wing segments. Salt and pepper generously.
- Over a medium charcoal fire, cook wing segments approximately 30 to 40 minutes, basting with the Lemon Butter Sauce.

Sausage Pastry Turnovers

Betsy White   4 dozen

1 cup butter
2 packages (3 ounce) cream cheese
2 cups flour
½ teaspoon salt
1 pound sausage, uncooked (hot or mild)
paprika

- Preheat oven to 425 degrees.
- Blend butter, cream cheese, flour and salt together. Cover and chill pastry for an hour or more. The resting period makes a crisper pastry.
- Let stand at room temperature for 30 minutes before rolling. Roll out thin on a floured pastry cloth. Cut into 2-inch rounds.
- Place a dab of sausage on each round. Fold over and press the edges together with a fork. These should look like miniature turnovers. Sprinkle with paprika and place on an ungreased cookie sheet.
- Bake for 20 minutes. Serve warm.

Hint: These are worth the time to make. Double the recipe and freeze in small plastic bags. They may be baked without thawing and are ready for instant company.

Ham Squares

JoAnn Arneson   50 squares

8 slices packaged ham
2 tablespoons prepared horseradish
1 teaspoon Worcestershire sauce
½ teaspoon seasoning salt
⅛ teaspoon pepper
1 package (8 ounce) cream cheese

- Place six of the ham slices separately on a flat surface, reserving 2 slices.
- Mix the remaining ingredients thoroughly. Spread two teaspoons of the cream cheese mixture over each slice of ham.
- Stack three pieces of the ham together. Repeat for remaining pieces. Top each of the two stacks with the remaining two slices of ham. Cut into bite-size squares. Place a toothpick in each square and refrigerate until time to serve.

Hint: It is important to have the ham on a flat surface while spreading the cream mixture to prevent the filling from oozing.

Caviar Spread

Deserves a silver tray!

Pat Taliaferro   16 servings

1 package (8 ounce) cream cheese
(nonfat optional), softened
2 teaspoons fresh lemon juice
2 tablespoons onion, minced
3 tablespoons nonfat sour cream
¼ teaspoon onion salt
1 jar (2 ounce) black lumpfish caviar
lemon slices, cut thin and halved
parsley sprigs
cocktail toast

- Blend cream cheese with lemon juice, onion, sour cream and salt. Spread ½ to ¾ inch thick on a 6 or 8-inch serving tray.
- Drain caviar well and spread evenly on top. Garnish edges with thin lemon slices and sprigs of parsley. Chill.
- Serve cold with crisp cocktail toasts.

Shrimp Spread

Debbie Ritter   15 to 20 servings

2 packages (8 ounce) cream cheese,
softened
1 teaspoon Louisiana hot sauce
⅛ teaspoon cayenne pepper
¼ teaspoon garlic powder
¼ teaspoon onion powder
2 teaspoons mustard seed
1 teaspoon celery seed
1 ½ tablespoons Worcestershire
sauce
¾ cup green onions, chopped
½ cup pimientos, chopped
1 cup cooked shrimp, chopped

• Cream together first eight ingredients. Add remaining ingredients. Chill two hours.

• Serve in a mound, surrounded with rye party bread. Delicious used as a filling for avocado halves. May be doubled easily.

Salmon Mousse

Laura Lewis   2 ½ cups

1 pound poached salmon, or 2 cans
(7 ½ ounce) red sockeye
4 ounces smoked salmon
1 medium scallion, minced
1 small shallot, minced
2 ½ tablespoons fresh lemon juice
½ teaspoon thyme
¼ teaspoon ground black pepper
½ teaspoon cayenne pepper
4 tablespoons unsalted butter,
softened
1 tablespoon fresh dill, coarsely
chopped
2 teaspoons capers, drained
1 ounce salmon roe for garnish
(optional)

• Combine the salmon, scallion, shallot, lemon juice, thyme and peppers in a food processor and pulse until blended.

• Add the butter, dill and capers and process until smooth. Transfer to a serving bowl and garnish with dill sprigs and salmon roe.

• Serve as a spread with crackers or toasts. This makes a lovely addition to a canapé tray.

Crab Stuffed Mushroom Caps

Sandra Williams   4 to 6 servings

16 shiitake mushroom caps, fresh or dried
1 unbeaten egg white
1 cup fresh crabmeat, shredded
1 teaspoon cornstarch
½ teaspoon ground ginger
1 teaspoon sherry
1 teaspoon salt

Calories per serving: 44
Saturated Fat 0 g
Cholesterol 17 mg
Total Fat 0 g (0% of Calories)
Sodium 565 mg

- If using dried shiitakes, soak in boiling water for 20 minutes, drain and squeeze dry.
- In medium bowl, mix egg white with crabmeat. Stir in cornstarch, ginger, sherry and salt.
- Stuff the mushroom caps with the crab filling. Arrange mushrooms in a steamer (or a plate raised above the water in a large pot).
- Steam fresh mushrooms for 20 minutes, until the caps begin to shrivel. Steam rehydrated caps only 10 minutes.

A delicacy from Oklahoma's own Lost Creek Mushroom Farm in Perkins.

Hot Lobster Dip

A real hit!

Jean Fishburne   12 servings

1 package (8 ounce) cream cheese
½ cup Sauterne wine
1 teaspoon sugar
1 teaspoon mustard
1 garlic clove, finely chopped
1 teaspoon onion, grated
¼ cup mayonnaise
salt and pepper to taste
1 package (8 ounce) frozen or fresh cooked lobster or crab

- In a saucepan, melt cream cheese over low heat until soft. Add remaining ingredients, leaving the lobster or crab until last. Mix gently. Adjust seasonings.
- Serve hot in a chafing dish with pita toast, French bread chunks or crackers.

Bleu Crab Fondue

Feodora Steward   12 to 15 servings

½ cup white wine
1 package (8 ounce) cream cheese, cubed
8 ounces cooked crabmeat
1 tablespoon chives, minced
3 ounces bleu cheese, crumbled

- Pour wine into a one-quart oven-proof dish. Heat until bubbly; add cream cheese.

- Cook uncovered for two minutes or until cheese melts, stirring once or twice.

- Blend in crabmeat and chives, cooking uncovered for 30 seconds. Gently toss in bleu cheese and heat one minute or until fondue is very hot.

Hint: Use artichoke hearts, apple slices or raw mushroom slices for dipping.

Feodora de Grasse Steward has been the piccolo player with the symphony for many years. After the flute and piccolo, her second love is dreaming up culinary originals.

Spicy Cocktail Beef

Adeanya Hunt   25 servings

7 pound beef roast, lean
1 bay leaf
1 tablespoon marjoram
1 tablespoon oregano
1 tablespoon summer savory
1 tablespoon cracked pepper
1 tablespoon rosemary
1 tablespoon garlic powder
salt and pepper to taste
party pumpernickel bread

MUSTARD SAUCE
2 tablespoons hot dry mustard
1 cup cider vinegar
2 eggs, beaten
1 cup sugar
pinch of salt

- Place roast in a large pot and add enough water to come halfway up on the meat. Add all other ingredients except salt and pepper. Simmer, covered, for about 8 hours.

- Remove roast from the broth and place on a platter. Salt and pepper sparingly. Shred the meat with two forks. Serve on pumpernickel or rye bread with Mustard Sauce (see below).

- At least one day before using the sauce, mix the mustard and vinegar in a tightly covered jar. Shake until thoroughly mixed and let stand overnight in the refrigerator.

- Serving Day: Place the sugar in the top of a double boiler over simmering water. Add the eggs, mustard mixture and salt. Cook and stir until mixture is thick enough to coat the spoon. Serve in a sauce boat to accompany Spicy Cocktail Beef. This keeps well in the refrigerator. Serve warm.

Hint: This recipe is good doubled or tripled. The sauce is also good on egg rolls.

Champagne Punch

Multiply for a crowd!

Helen S. Fay

18 cups

2 bottles (1 liter) ginger ale, chilled
1 can (6 ounce) frozen lemonade,
thawed and undiluted
12 maraschino cherries
1 can (12 ounce) frozen orange
juice concentrate, diluted
1 bottle (750 ml) dry champagne,
chilled

- Pour 1 bottle of ginger ale and lemonade concentrate into an 11-cup ring mold. Add cherries and freeze until firm. Unmold ice ring in a punch bowl.
- Add remaining ginger ale, orange juice and champagne. Stir well.

Bravo to the Omniplex Science Museum in Oklahoma City. From aerospace to beautiful gardens, experiencing Omniplex is time well spent. A fascinating collection of early clocks from the Fay family of Norman is on display at Omniplex.

Strawberry Lemonade Punch

Perfect for a bridal shower!

Helen S. Fay

20 Servings

1 can (6 ounce) frozen lemonade,
thawed and undiluted
1 can (6 ounce) frozen limeade,
thawed and undiluted
1 can (6 ounce) frozen orange
juice concentrate, thawed and
undiluted
2 packages (10 ounce) frozen sliced
strawberries, thawed
3 cups cold water
2 bottles (1 liter) ginger ale, chilled

- Combine first 5 ingredients. Add ginger ale and stir gently. May easily be increased for larger groups.

Frozen Banana Punch

Jacquelyn Stengel

48 servings

3 ¼ cups sugar
6 cups water
6 bananas, mashed
1 can (46 ounce) pineapple juice
½ cup fresh lemon juice
1 can (6 ounce) frozen orange juice, undiluted
1 bottle (2 liter) ginger ale

- Boil sugar and water for 4 minutes; cool. In a one-gallon freezer container, combine sugar syrup, bananas, pineapple juice, lemon juice and orange juice concentrate. Freeze.

- To serve: place frozen fruit mixture in a punch bowl. Add ginger ale and stir to a slushy consistency.

Cranberry Punch

A real crowd pleaser!

Billie Hodgell

12 to 15 servings

½ gallon cranberry juice
2 cinnamon sticks
1 cup orange juice
½ cup lemon juice
½ cup sugar, to taste

- Heat cranberry juice and cinnamon sticks to boiling. Remove from heat and cool.

- Remove cinnamon sticks and add orange and lemon juices. Add sugar to taste. May be served hot or cold and multiplied for larger groups.

Calories per serving: 124
Saturated Fat 0 g
Cholesterol 0 mg
Total Fat 0 g (0% of Calories)
Sodium 3 mg

Southern Iced Coffee Punch

Perfect for a reception!

Donna Miller

24 servings

1 gallon strong coffee
1 cup sugar
1 quart fudge ripple ice cream
1 ¼ cups dark rum
4 pints half & half

- Make coffee in advance; add sugar and refrigerate. Just before serving, add rum and half and half to coffee.

- Pour over ice cream in punch bowl. May be easily doubled for large groups.

Hot Spiced Cider

Jane Baker   18 servings

**4 quarts apple cider
1 cup orange juice
⅓ cup sugar
2 teaspoons grated orange peel
1 teaspoon whole allspice
½ teaspoon mace
¼ teaspoon salt
1 teaspoon coriander seed
2 teaspoons whole cloves
2 tablespoons cinnamon sticks,
broken into bits
1 cup pineapple juice, optional**

- Combine all ingredients in a large saucepan. Cover and heat to boiling. Reduce heat and simmer for 30 minutes.
- Strain and serve hot.

> Calories per serving: 146
> Saturated Fat 0 g
> Cholesterol 0 mg
> Total Fat 0 g (0% of Calories)
> Sodium 34 mg

Orange Smoothie

Russ Frazee   4 servings

**1 can (6 ounce) frozen orange juice
concentrate, undiluted
½ cup water
½ cup milk
⅓ cup sugar (or less)
1 teaspoon vanilla extract
3 cups ice, crushed
1 cup vanilla frozen nonfat yogurt**

- Mix all ingredients in a blender for 30 seconds.

> Calories per serving: 215
> Saturated Fat 0 g
> Cholesterol 2 mg
> Total Fat 1 g (3% of Calories)
> Sodium 65 mg

Tropical Ice

Donna Miller   4 servings

**4 ripe bananas, peeled
½ cup sugar
4 oranges, juice only
4 limes, juice only
½ cup water**

> Calories per serving: 296
> Saturated Fat 0 g
> Cholesterol 0 mg
> Total Fat 1 g (3% of Calories)
> Sodium 3 mg

- In a large bowl, mash the bananas well and combine with the sugar. Stir in the orange and lime juices and water. Stir until thoroughly mixed. Pour into individual serving cups and freeze about 4 hours. Or make ahead and thaw until slushy before serving. Garnish with an orange or lime slice.

Frozen Margaritas

For a taste of South of the Border!

Carole Almond   12 servings

1 pint **tequila**
1 pint **Triple Sec**
1 cup **Rose's lime juice**
2 cans (12 ounce) **frozen lemonade,**
thawed
ice cubes
lime wedges
coarse salt

- In a large bowl or pitcher, mix tequila, Triple Sec, lime juice and lemonade concentrate.

- In a blender, combine 1 cup of mixture and 3 cups ice cubes. Blend until smooth.

- Serve in glasses after rubbing the rims with a lime wedge and dipping in salt. Then prepare refills.

Rum Mint Cooler

Barbara Messenbaugh   24 servings

2 cups **sugar**
2 cups **water**
4 cups **fresh mint**
1 can (12 ounce) **frozen orange**
juice, thawed
1 can (12 ounce) **frozen lemonade,**
thawed
rum

Calories per serving: 187
Saturated Fat 0 g
Cholesterol 0 mg
Total Fat 0 g (0% of Calories)
Sodium 36 mg

- Boil water and sugar together until sugar is dissolved. Remove from burner and add fresh mint. Cover and let steep 30 minutes. Strain through cheesecloth then discard mint.

- Add orange juice and lemonade to mint mixture and stir. Store in refrigerator until ready to serve.

- To serve, mix ⅓ cup mint concentrate to ⅔ cup soda. Use tall glasses with lots of ice. Add 1 large jigger of rum per drink.

Citrus Bourbon Slush

Addictive!

Verna Miller   40 servings

7 cups water
4 tea bags
⅔ cup sugar
1 can (6 ounce) frozen orange juice
1 can (12 ounce) frozen lemonade
1 ½ cups bourbon

- Boil 2 cups water. Brew tea bags for at least 10 minutes. Add remaining 5 cups of water.
- Mix all ingredients with tea and stir well.
- Place in freezer, stirring several times in the first day.
- Serve in old fashioned glasses with spoons. This will keep in the freezer indefinitely.

Brandy Ice for a Crowd

Really a dessert!

Beth Shumway   72 servings

3 gallons vanilla ice cream
48 ounces brandy (cognac)
6 ounces Triple Sec
6 ounces banana liqueur
6 ounces Kahlua

- Soften ice cream. Mix with all other ingredients.
- Store in freezer using air tight containers. Stir before serving.

Developed by Marion Wilson and Elaine Shepherd for Lake Aluma gatherings. Try it at your next neighborhood party. Applause to Mrs. Shumway for founding and directing the Prairie Dance Theater.

BREADS

V. VANN

BREADS

THE ROUND BARN

The Round Barn is one of the most frequently visited historic sites on Oklahoma Route 66. Built by W.H. Ordor in 1898, this unusual structure was placed on the National Register of Historic Places in 1977. Sixty feet in diameter and 43 feet from the foundation to the peak of the dome, the barn is built entirely from native burr oak, shaped while green and held in a proper curve until dried. In 1988, a portion of the roof blew off in a wind storm and its future was in jeopardy until the Arcadia Historical and Preservation Society came to the rescue. Luke Robison, a retired carpenter, headed a crew of volunteers who restored the barn, using 1898 tools and materials.

Will Rogers Hotel Cinnamon Bread

Let's stop for Cinnamon Bread!

Cinderella Groce   2 loaves

¾ cup butter, softened
½ cup sugar
4 cups flour
1 ½ teaspoon salt
1 cake yeast
1 cup milk
3 eggs

- Cream sugar and butter together. Sift flour and salt into creamed mixture and beat in with spoon.
- Scald milk and cool to lukewarm before mixing with yeast. Pour milk and beaten eggs into the creamed mixture. Stir together.
- Form dough into ball and place in oiled bowl. Brush top with melted butter. Let rise until half again the original size. Punch down, fold over and knead on a floured board. Roll into two 10-inch squares.

CINNAMON FILLING
3 tablespoons butter, melted
¼ cup sugar
1 teaspoon cinnamon

- Combine ingredients and spread mixture on dough. Fold ends of dough over and seal edges in center. Tuck ends up if necessary before placing in two well-greased loaf pans. Let rise again.
- Bake for 45 minutes in preheated 400 degree oven.

Humorist, philosopher, actor, philanthropist - all of these describe Will Rogers, the onetime Cherokee Kid, but above all he was the typical American and Oklahoma's own.

The world was his audience, but he never lost the common touch. Many stories were told about Rogers refusing to wear a dinner coat at formal affairs, but he finally gave in and ordered a tuxedo. "I'm getting to be like a fireman," he said. "Every time I hear the word 'dinner', I slide into my dinner clothes and dash off to attend it."

The Will Rogers Hotel in Claremore is famous for its Cinnamon Bread and is currently being restored and preserved. The hotel, located on Route 66, has provided a cherished chapter in Oklahoma's history.

Seven Grain Bread

Marion DeVore   2 loaves

1 ½ cups boiling water
1 cup seven grain cereal
6 tablespoons safflower oil
½ cup honey
2 teaspoons lite salt (optional)
½ cup warm water
2 packages dry yeast
½ cup egg substitute
5 ½ cups whole wheat flour,
divided

Calories per serving: 176
Saturated Fat 0 g
Cholesterol 0 mg
Total Fat 4 g (21% of Calories)
Sodium 94 mg

- Pour boiling water over the seven grain cereal in a large mixing bowl. Dissolve the yeast in warm water. When the cereal mix is lukewarm, add the yeast and all remaining ingredients except one cup of flour. Beat vigorously for two minutes. Work in remaining flour.

- Divide the dough in half and spread into the bottoms of two oiled loaf pans, or five 3x6-inch pans. Let rise until double and bake at 375 degrees for 50 minutes.

Salt Free Pecan Yeast Bread

Jeannine F. Spencer   2 loaves

1 tablespoon dry yeast
1 cup warm water
1 cup milk
½ cup butter
4 cups flour
½ cup pecans, finely chopped
2 eggs

- Dissolve yeast in water. Heat milk and butter just until butter melts. Cool to lukewarm. Add to yeast. Add flour and pecans and eggs. Mix well and knead for 10 minutes. Let rise, punch down and let rise again. Each of these risings takes about an hour.

- Preheat oven to 375 degrees.

- Divide dough into two loaves. Let rise until it doubles in size. Bake 40 minutes or until loaves sound hollow when tapped.

G rand Champion Bread Winner at the Oklahoma Pecan Growers Food Show!

Sesame Loaves

For a special Italian dinner

Wanda Cook   2 loaves

2 cups warm water
2 packages yeast
1 tablespoon sugar
2 teaspoons salt
5 ½ cups flour, sifted
1 egg white, beaten
1 tablespoon water
2 tablespoons sesame seeds

- Measure water into large bowl. Sprinkle yeast and stir until dissolved.

- Add sugar, salt and 3 cups flour. Stir to mix and beat until smooth and shiny. Add 2 ½ cups flour.

- Turn dough onto lightly floured board and knead for 5 minutes. Shape into ball and place in large, greased bowl, turning once to grease top of dough. Cover. Let rise in warm place, free of drafts, until double in bulk, about ½ hour. Punch dough down and divide in half. Let rest 5 minutes.

- Shape each half into a ball and place 4 inches apart on a greased baking sheet. With a sharp knife, slash tops of loaves ¼ inch deep in desired pattern. Cover and let rise in warm place until a little more than doubled in bulk, about ½ hour.

- Mix beaten egg with water, spread on top of loaves and sprinkle with seeds.

- Bake at 425 degrees for 15 minutes.

Originally published in the **Daily Oklahoman** forty years ago. But just as good today.

Sourdough Rye

Frances Robinson   2 loaves

2 packages dry yeast
3 ¼ cups warm water (100 to 115
degrees)
6 cups flour, approximately
2 cups rye flour
2 teaspoons salt
1 tablespoon caraway seeds
1 ½ teaspoons poppy seeds
2 tablespoons butter, melted
3 tablespoons granulated sugar
⅛ cup cornmeal
1 egg, lightly beaten with
1 tablespoon water

- Four days ahead of breadmaking, prepare the "starter". Combine 1 package yeast, 2 cups warm water, and 2 cups flour in a plastic bowl or container. Cover tightly and let stand at room temperature for 2 days. Refrigerate for at least another day.

- The day before preparing the dough, combine 1 cup of starter, the rye flour, and 1 cup warm water in a bowl. Cover with plastic wrap and let stand at room temperature overnight.

- Stir down the dough and add the second package of yeast, dissolved in ¼ cup warm water, salt, caraway seeds, poppy seeds, butter and sugar. Add up to 4 cups flour, 1 cup at a time, to make a stiff but workable dough. Knead for 10 to 12 minutes, then shape into a ball. Place in a buttered bowl, turning to coat the dough with the butter. Cover and let rise in a warm, draft free place until doubled in bulk, about 2 hours.

- Punch down and divide the dough in half. Shape into two round loaves and place on buttered baking sheets generously sprinkled with cornmeal. Cover and let rise again until doubled in bulk, about 1 hour.

- Preheat oven to 375 degrees.

- Brush loaves with egg wash and bake 30 minutes or until lightly browned and the loaves sound hollow when tapped with the knuckles.

- Cool, covered with towels, to prevent the crust from hardening.

Hint: This provides more sourdough starter than needed for this recipe. To keep it going, replenish with equal parts of warm water and flour. Let stand again at room temperature. Repeat this process each time the starter is used. The childhood memories of smelling this bread bake make it all worthwhile.

French Bread

Pain de Ménage

Harriette G. Orbach   4 baguettes

2 packages dry yeast
3 teaspoons salt
1 ½ tablespoons sugar
3 cups lukewarm water
6 cups flour
sesame seeds, fennel seeds, poppy
seeds or caraway seeds.

Calories per serving: 118
Saturated Fat 0 g
Cholesterol 0 mg
Total Fat 0 g (0% of Calories)
Sodium 295 mg

- In a large bowl, dissolve yeast in water with salt and sugar. Gradually add flour, 1 cup at a time, until mixture absorbs no more flour.

- Knead the dough on a floured board or marble slab until it is slightly elastic, usually 3 or 4 minutes. Place dough in ungreased bowl, cover with plastic wrap and a dish towel and let rise for 1 hour in a warmed, then turned off oven.

- Punch down and let rise 45 minutes. Butter baguette pans and sprinkle with corn meal.

- Without working the dough too much, divide into 4 parts and shape into baguettes. Let rise another 45 minutes.

- Brush lightly with egg mixed with a dash of water and sprinkle with seeds. Let rise 45 minutes.

- Preheat oven to 450 degrees. Bake 5 minutes at 450 degrees, or 25 minutes at 375 degrees. Slice diagonally.

- May be frozen. After baking, cool, wrap in foil and freeze. To thaw, place bread in 400 degree oven (do not preheat). When temperature is reached, bread should be thawed.

Quick Honey Wheat Bran Rolls

Erick Honey Festival   3 dozen

½ cup honey
½ teaspoon salt
3 cups warm water
2 packages dry yeast
½ cup vegetable oil
1 cup wheat bran
6 ¼ cups bread flour
melted butter and honey to glaze

Calories per serving: 139
Saturated Fat 0 g
Cholesterol 1 mg
Total Fat 4 g (25% of Calories)
Sodium 37 mg

- In a large mixing bowl, dissolve honey and salt in warm water, then stir in the yeast until it is dissolved.
- Add oil and wheat bran. Stir until mixed. Add flour and mix until well blended.
- Shape into rolls and let rise 30 minutes.
- Bake at 400 degrees for 10 minutes, then reduce heat to 350 degrees and bake until brown. Brush with melted butter mixed with a little honey.

Each year the town of Erick in western Oklahoma celebrates its Honey Festival. This recipe was a Grand Champion Winner and how right they were!

Homemade Bagels

Frances Robinson

12 bagels

1 package dry yeast
½ cup very warm water
⅛ teaspoon sugar
1 cup warm water
3 scant tablespoons sugar
1 scant tablespoon salt
4 ½ cups unbleached flour,
approximately
large pot of water
1 teaspoon salt
1 tablespoon sugar

Calories per serving: 181
Saturated Fat 0 g
Cholesterol 0 mg
Total Fat 0 g (0% of Calories)
Sodium 587 mg

- **Remove the oven racks** and pre-heat oven to 350 degrees.

- Dissolve yeast in the ½ cup warm water, with ⅛ teaspoon sugar, to proof.

- Pour remaining 1 cup warm water into large mixer bowl and add sugar and salt.

- When yeast water bubbles, add to mixer bowl. Use a dough hook if available. With mixer running, gradually add just enough flour for dough to form a sticky ball. Remove dough to a lightly floured board and knead until smooth and satiny, about 10 minutes. Cover with a damp towel and let rise for 30 minutes.

- Reduce the dough by rolling with your hands. Divide into four equal parts and then divide each part into three or four equal sized pieces. Roll each piece of dough with your hands to resemble a rope as thick as two fingers. Stretching the dough slightly as you work, form a circle, pinching the dough together with your thumb to seal. Reshape, if necessary after sealing. Place bagels on a wooden bread board, cover with a towel, and let rise for 20 minutes.

- Bring a large wide pot of water to a boil. Add the rest of the salt and sugar. When the bagels have risen, drop into the boiling water being careful that they do not touch. Keep water at a simmer or below. Cook bagels 45 to 50 seconds on each side, turning with a slotted spoon. Remove to the bread board to cool.

- Place cool and dry bagels on the oven rack and bake about 10 minutes. Turn the bagels and continue baking until lightly browned, about 8 to 10 additional minutes. Do not overbake.

Cheesy Onion Burger Buns

Top winner at the first Watonga Cheese Festival in 1976!

Clella Lookabaugh   20 Buns

6 ½ cups flour, unsifted
3 tablespoons sugar
1 ½ teaspoons salt
2 packages active dry yeast
2 tablespoons butter, softened
2 cups very hot tap water
1 ½ cups sharp Cheddar cheese, grated
¼ cup onion, finely chopped

- In a large bowl, thoroughly mix 2 cups flour, sugar, salt and undissolved dry yeast. Add butter. Gradually add hot tap water to the dry ingredients and beat 2 minutes at medium speed of mixer.

- Add 1 cup of flour or enough flour to make a thick batter. Beat at high speed 2 minutes.

- Stir in cheese, onion and enough additional flour to make a soft dough. Turn out onto lightly floured board and knead until smooth and elastic, about 8 to 10 minutes.

- Place dough in a greased bowl, turning to grease top. Cover. Let rise in a warm place away from draft until doubled in bulk, about 1 hour.

- Punch dough down and turn out onto lightly floured board. Divide the dough into 20 equal pieces. Form each piece into a smooth ball. Place the balls 2 inches apart on greased baking sheets. Cover. Let rise until doubled in bulk, about 45 minutes.

- Preheat oven to 400 degrees. Bake buns 15 to 20 minutes or until done. Cool on wire racks.

Overnight Cinnamon Rolls

Lou Shepherd   6 dozen

ROLLS
1 package dry yeast
½ cup warm water
1 teaspoon sugar
2 cups very hot water
¾ cup sugar
1 teaspoon salt
½ cup vegetable oil
6 cups flour
2 eggs

Late afternoon:

- Dissolve yeast in warm water. Add sugar and set aside.

- In the meantime, mix the very hot water, sugar, salt and oil. Cool to lukewarm.

- Add 3 cups flour, eggs and yeast mixture. Beat well. Add enough more flour to make a soft dough. Let rise. After dough doubles in volume, punch down and let rise again.

- Divide dough into 4 parts. Roll each into a rectangle. Spread with butter, cinnamon and sugar. Roll up and cut into slices 1 inch thick. Place in pans coated with cooking spray. Let rise, uncovered, overnight.

In the morning:

- Preheat oven to 350 degrees. Bake prepared rolls 15 to 18 minutes. Ice with powdered sugar glaze while still warm.

POWDERED SUGAR GLAZE
1 ½ cups powdered sugar, sifted
3 tablespoons water
1 teaspoon vanilla or almond extract

- Combine ingredients and drizzle over warm cinnamon rolls.

Kolaches

A Czech Festival favorite!

Yvette Fleckinger 4 dozen

½ cup lukewarm water
1 tablespoon sugar
2 packages yeast
6 ½ cups flour
1 cup butter
¾ cup sugar
1 teaspoon salt
3 eggs
1 can (12 ounce) evaporated milk, scalded

- Mix lukewarm water (about 115 degrees) and 1 tablespoon sugar with yeast and enough flour to make a batter of pancake consistency. Let rise until double in volume.
- Cream butter, ¾ cup sugar, salt and eggs. Stir in scalded milk; let cool to lukewarm. Add yeast mixture to butter and sugar mixture. Add enough flour to make a soft dough. Again let rise until double in volume. Punch down.
- Drop rounded teaspoons of dough onto lightly floured surface. Shape into round balls. Place on greased baking pans. Let rise.
- Preheat oven to 350 degrees. Make a depression in center of dough balls. Place filling in depression and sprinkle with topping. Let rise until light.
- Bake 15 minutes or until light brown.

APRICOT KOLACHE FILLING
1 pound dried apricots
1 cup sugar
2 tablespoons flour

- Cover apricots with water and cook until tender. Drain. Add sugar and flour, stirring until apricots are crushed. Cool.

KOLACHE CRUNCH TOPPING
½ cup flour
½ cup sugar
1 tablespoon butter
⅓ teaspoon cinnamon, optional

- Mix all ingredients until crumbly.

Surprise Corn Muffins

Enid's new twist to an old favorite!

Betty Elton   12 muffins

1 cup flour
1 cup yellow corn meal
¼ cup sugar
1 tablespoon baking powder
1 teaspoon red pepper flakes
1 egg
½ cup plus 1 tablespoon milk
¼ cup vegetable oil
1 can (10 ounces) creamed corn
¼ cup jalapeño pepper jelly

- Preheat oven to 375 degrees. Coat muffin tins with vegetable spray.
- In large bowl, mix flour, corn meal, sugar, baking powder and pepper flakes.
- Whisk together egg, milk, oil and corn. Pour liquid mixture over dry ingredients and stir lightly, using no more than 15-20 strokes.
- Fill each muffin cup ½ full with batter. With back of teaspoon, make small depression in center of each muffin and drop in one teaspoon of jelly. Divide remaining batter over muffins to cover jelly.
- Bake for 25 minutes or until light golden brown. Let muffins rest in pan for two minutes, ease onto a plate and cool for about twenty minutes.

Indian Territory Cornbread

Betty Schmahl Kay   6 to 8 servings

2 cups yellow corn meal
2 teaspoons baking powder
½ teaspoon baking soda
2 teaspoons salt
4 eggs, beaten
1 ½ cups buttermilk
1 cup water
1 tablespoon vegetable shortening

- Preheat oven to 425 degrees.
- Sift together dry ingredients. Combine eggs, buttermilk and water; slowly stir into cornmeal mixture just until dry ingredients are moistened.
- Melt shortening in a 9-inch cast iron skillet in a 400 degree oven for 3 minutes or until very hot. Sprinkle a few grains of corn meal in bottom of skillet before pouring batter. Bake 35 minutes or until lightly browned.

Broccoli Bread

Florence N. Ratzlaff   6 servings

1 box frozen chopped broccoli,
thawed and drained
1 box Jiffy cornbread mix
½ cup butter, melted
1 large onion, chopped
1 teaspoon salt (or less)
4 eggs
6 ounces cottage cheese, small curd

- Preheat oven to 375 degrees. Coat 7x10-inch or square pan with vegetable spray.
- In mixing bowl combine eggs, salt, melted butter, onion and cottage cheese and stir until mixed. Add cornbread mix, chopped broccoli and mix together.
- Pour into prepared pan and bake 35 to 40 minutes. Cut into squares. Serve as a casserole or spoon bread.

Date Nut Loaf

Awarded Best in Show at Tulsa State Fair

Freida Biddle   12 servings

4 eggs
1 cup sugar
½ cup vegetable oil
1 teaspoon salt
1 cup flour
8 ounces whole, pitted dates
2 cups pecan halves

- Grease and flour a loaf pan. Do not preheat oven.
- Combine eggs, sugar, and oil; beat well. Add remaining ingredients; mix just until moistened. Pour into prepared pan. Place in a cold oven. Set oven at 300 degrees and bake for 2 hours.

Apricot Almond Bread

Gladys Schmahl   12 servings

1 ½ cups dried apricots
1 ½ cups boiling water
2 tablespoons butter
1 cup sugar
1 teaspoon salt
1 egg, well beaten
1 cup whole wheat flour
1 ½ cups pastry flour
1 teaspoon soda
1 cup almonds, finely chopped
1 teaspoon orange extract

- Preheat oven to 350 degrees. Grease and flour one loaf pan.
- Sift flours and soda together.
- To apricots, add water, butter, sugar and salt. Blend well and then add to other ingredients.
- Turn into prepared pan and bake 1 hour 15 minutes.

Hint: Delicious served with cream cheese thinned with apricot brandy.

Lemon Saffron Tea Bread

From An Herbal Affair in Sand Springs!

Malea L. Barber

12 servings

1 cup whole wheat flour
1 ¾ cups flour
2 teaspoons baking powder
¼ teaspoon baking soda
⅓ cup butter, softened
2 eggs
¼ teaspoon saffron, crushed
¾ cup honey
1 ½ tablespoons lemon rind, freshly grated
¾ cup milk

- Preheat oven to 350 degrees. Butter a 9x5 inch loaf pan and line the bottom with waxed paper. Butter again.
- Mix wheat flour, flour, baking powder and baking soda; set aside.
- In a separate bowl, cream butter. Add honey, eggs, lemon rind, saffron and milk. Mix well and let stand 5 minutes.
- Slowly add the milk mixture to the dry ingredients, mixing well after each addition. Pour the batter into the prepared pan and bake 50 to 60 minutes or until toothpick inserted in center comes out clean.
- Remove from oven and run a knife around the edges of the bread. Turn the bread out onto a wire rack that is standing on waxed paper. Drizzle topping (see below) over bread.

LEMON TOPPING
2 tablespoons lemon juice
⅓ cup honey
1 teaspoon lemon rind, freshly grated

- Mix lemon juice and honey together. Drizzle over bread while it is still hot. Sprinkle grated lemon rind over surface of bread. Place bread on a baking sheet and place under a broiler for 1 to 2 minutes or until the top caramelizes. Watch carefully to avoid burning. Cool bread before serving.

Calories per serving: 271
Saturated Fat 4 g
Cholesterol 51 mg
Total Fat 7 g (23% of Calories)
Sodium 148 mg

Blueberry Muffins

For the diet conscious!

David Ward   1 dozen

½ cup whole wheat flour
1 cup flour
¼ cup corn meal
2 teaspoons baking powder
2 teaspoons powdered saccharin
½ teaspoon grated lemon peel
⅛ teaspoon cinnamon
⅛ teaspoon nutmeg
2 tablespoons corn oil
1 egg
1 teaspoon lemon extract
1 cup milk
1 cup blueberries

- Preheat oven to 375 degrees. Coat muffin tins with vegetable spray.

- Combine dry ingredients. Beat together oil and egg, then add lemon extract and milk. Mix with dry ingredients and fold in blueberries. Spoon into 12 muffin cups.

- Bake for 25 minutes. Best when served warm.

Hint: Can be topped with all fruit blueberry jam.

Calories per serving: 114
Saturated Fat 1 g
Cholesterol 20 mg
Total Fat 4 g (30% of Calories)
Sodium 75 mg

Virginia's Sweet Potato Muffins

Virginia Edwards   2 dozen

½ cup butter
1 ¼ cups sugar
2 eggs
1 ¼ cups sweet potatoes, cooked and mashed
1 ½ cups unbleached flour
2 teaspoons baking powder
¼ teaspoon salt
1 teaspoon cinnamon
¼ teaspoon nutmeg
1 cup milk
¼ cup pecans or walnuts, chopped
½ cup raisins, chopped

- Preheat oven to 400 degrees. Coat muffin pans with vegetable spray.

- Cream butter and sugar. Add eggs and mashed sweet potatoes, mixing well.

- Sift dry ingredients. Add to sweet potato mixture, alternately with milk. Do not over-mix. Fold in nuts and raisins. Fill muffin tins ⅔ full.

- Bake for about 25 minutes.

Hint: These are perfect for a tea. Just use mini muffin tins.

Scrumptious Pumpkin Muffins

Pauline Morgan   18 muffins

½ cup butter, softened
1 cup sugar
2 eggs
1 cup canned pumpkin
2 cups flour, divided
2 teaspoons baking powder
¼ teaspoon salt
1 teaspoon cinnamon
¼ teaspoon nutmeg
1 cup milk
½ cup pecans, chopped
½ cup raisins

- Preheat oven to 400 degrees. Grease muffin pans.
- Cream butter; gradually add sugar, beating well. Add eggs, one at a time, then the pumpkin, beating well after every addition.
- Sift together 1 ¾ cups flour, baking powder, salt and spices.
- Add flour mixture to creamed ingredients, alternately with milk, beginning and ending with flour mixture. Beat well after each addition.
- Dredge pecans and raisins in remaining flour and fold into batter.
- Spoon batter into greased muffin pans, filling ⅔ full.
- Bake 25 minutes or until golden brown.

A special muffin for Halloween, Thanksgiving and Christmas. Delicious served with hot spiced cider in the afternoons. A favorite at the turn of the century at homes near The Round Barn in Arcadia.

Championship Muffins

Jean Fishburne   100 mini muffins

4 cups flour
2 ½ cups sugar
4 teaspoons baking soda
4 teaspoons cinnamon
1 teaspoon salt
4 cups apples, peeled and grated
1 cup raisins (optional)
1 cup pecans, chopped
1 cup carrot, shredded
6 large eggs
2 cups vegetable oil
4 teaspoons vanilla extract

- Preheat oven to 350 degrees. Coat muffin pans with vegetable spray.
- In a large bowl, sift flour, sugar, soda, cinnamon and salt. Stir in apples, raisins, pecans and carrots.
- Combine eggs, oil and vanilla and mix thoroughly. Add to flour mixture and stir until just blended.
- Fill muffin tins ⅔ full and bake 15 minutes or until muffins spring to touch.
- Let cool 5 minutes on wire rack before removing.

45

Orange Biscuits

Gooey and Good!

Jean Petito   10 servings

⅓ cup orange juice
3 tablespoons butter
1 teaspoon grated orange rind
1 tablespoon lemon juice
¾ cup sugar
10 refrigerator biscuits, or homemade

- Preheat oven to 450 degrees; 425 degrees if using a glass pan.
- Melt butter and add orange juice, orange rind, lemon juice and sugar. Boil for 2 minutes.
- Pour into 8x8-inch pan. Place biscuits on top of mixture and bake 15 to 20 minutes. Do not over-bake.
- Turn pan upside down onto a serving plate. Serve warm.

Sunrise Coffee Cake

Karen Casabon   6 to 8 servings

2 eggs (or ½ cup egg substitute)
2 cups biscuit mix
⅓ cup sugar
⅔ cup milk
½ cup nuts, chopped

- Preheat oven to 400 degrees.
- Beat eggs until foamy.
- Combine biscuit mix and sugar. Add to eggs alternately with milk.
- Stir in nuts and spread in an 8-inch round glass baking dish.
- Bake for 25 minutes.

TOPPING
⅓ cup butter, melted
⅔ cup brown sugar
½ cup orange rind, grated
½ cup nuts, chopped
½ cup orange juice

- Mix butter and brown sugar and spread over top while warm.
- Sprinkle with rind and nuts. Pour orange juice over the top and place under broiler until bubbly. Serve warm.

Pecan Breakfast Bread

Grace Boulton   8 servings

2 cans crescent dinner rolls
2 tablespoons butter, softened
½ cup sugar
2 teaspoons cinnamon
¼ cup pecans, chopped

- Preheat oven to 375 degrees. Grease 9x5-inch loaf pan.
- Unroll crescents and separate into 16 triangles. Spread butter over each.
- Combine sugar, cinnamon and pecans. Sprinkle over triangles.
- Roll up triangles starting from wide end and rolling to opposite point. Place rolls point side down in prepared pan, forming 2 layers of 8 rolls each.
- Bake 35 to 40 minutes until golden brown. Remove from pan at once. Place right side up on serving platter.

HONEY TOPPING
2 tablespoons honey
¼ cup powdered sugar
2 tablespoons butter, softened
1 teaspoon vanilla extract
¼ cup pecans, chopped

- While bread is baking, combine all topping ingredients except pecans. Bring to a boil, stirring constantly. Remove from heat and stir in pecans. Cool slightly. Drizzle over baked rolls on serving platter.

Blueberry Sausage Breakfast Cake

Mattie Perryman   8 to 10 servings

2 cups flour
1 teaspoon baking powder
½ teaspoon baking soda
½ cup butter
¾ cup sugar
¼ cup brown sugar, packed
2 eggs
1 carton (8 ounce) sour cream
1 pound bulk pork sausage,
cooked and drained
1 cup blueberries, fresh or frozen
½ cup chopped pecans

- Preheat oven to 350 degrees.
- Stir together the flour, baking powder and baking soda and set aside.
- In the large mixer bowl, beat butter with mixer until light and fluffy. Add the sugars and beat until well creamed. Add eggs, one at a time, beating after each addition.
- Add the flour mixture and the sour cream alternately, beating after each addition. Fold in the sausage and berries.
- Spread batter evenly into an ungreased 13x9x2-inch pan and sprinkle with pecans.
- Bake for 35 to 40 minutes. Cool on a wire rack and serve with hot blueberry sauce.

HOT BLUEBERRY SAUCE
½ cup sugar
2 tablespoons cornstarch
½ cup water
2 cups blueberries, fresh or frozen
½ teaspoon lemon juice

- Mix first four ingredients well in a saucepan and cook over medium heat, stirring constantly, until thickened. Simmer 2 minutes.
- Remove from heat, add lemon juice, and cool slightly before spooning over cake.

Hint: Cake may be covered and refrigerated overnight before baking.

48

Irish Apple Potato Bread

A touch of old Ireland!

Barry Douglas   Serves 4

1 large potato, boiled and cooled
1 cup flour
1 pinch salt
2 medium cooking apples,
uncooked

Calories per serving: 262
Saturated Fat 0 g
Cholesterol 0 mg
Total Fat 1 g (3% of Calories)
Sodium 104 mg

- Mash the potato by hand until coarse but not lumpy. Add flour and salt and rub together until it resembles bread crumbs. Knead it until it forms a dough using a little water if needed.

- Sprinkle work top with flour and roll out the dough thinly.

- Peel and thinly slice apples and arrange them over half of dough area. Fold over other half of dough and seal.

- Coat frying pan with flour and preheat the pan (no oil needed). Cook bread until it is crisp and the apples are soft. There may be a burning odor but potato bread should not burn.

- When serving, open the pastry and add sugar and butter to taste.

Irish pianist Barry Douglas wrote from Paris, "A Black Bush Irish Whiskey goes down a treat with this, or even a Bailey's Irish Cream..."!

Veranika

Mennonite Community of Fairview

2 eggs, beaten
¼ teaspoon salt
½ cup whipping cream
2 ½ cups flour
vegetable oil for deep frying

- Place eggs, salt and whipping cream into a mixing bowl. Add flour and knead until a firm, workable dough is achieved. Dough should be elastic and not sticking to your hands.

- Roll out the dough on a floured board and cut into 4-inch squares, or cut with a large water glass or 13-ounce coffee can.

FILLING
2 cups cottage cheese (dry curd)
2 tablespoons cream
¼ teaspoon salt
¼ teaspoon pepper
2 eggs, beaten

- Mix all filling ingredients together and place a heaping spoonful of the cheese mixture in the middle of each round of dough. Fold the dough over and press the edges together.

- Heat cooking oil in a skillet and fry the veranika until brown on both sides. Serve with Sour Cream or Sweet Sauce.

SOUR CREAM SAUCE
2 medium onions, chopped
1 ½ cups sour cream
ham or bacon drippings
Salt to taste

- Sauté onions in the drippings until tender. Add the sour cream and salt. Heat to boiling. Serve hot over the veranika.

SWEET SAUCE
½ cup pancake syrup
½ cup whipping cream

- Heat syrup and whipping cream together and serve warm over veranikas.

Hint: Veranikas may also be cooked in boiling water instead of frying them.

Crusty Seed Sticks

Adeanya Hunt   20 sticks

1 can refrigerated biscuits
milk
1 ½ cups crisp rice cereal, crushed
2 tablespoons caraway seed, celery
seed, sesame seed or dill seed
2 teaspoons salt

- Preheat oven to 450 degrees.
- Cut biscuits in half. Roll each piece into a thin stick about 4 inches long. Brush with milk.
- Mix cereal crumbs, your choice of seed and salt. Roll sticks in mixture and place on cookie sheet.
- Bake for 10 minutes or until lightly browned. Good served with soup or salad.

Chickasaw Fry Bread

Tishomingo's Chickasaw Festival   16 pieces

1 package dry yeast
2 tablespoons sugar
1 tablespoon salt
2 cups warm water
4 to 5 cups flour
oil for deep fat frying

- Dissolve yeast, sugar and salt in warm water in a large bowl. Let stand for about 5 minutes. Add just enough flour to make the dough elastic (not stiff). Knead just enough to hold together.
- Oil the bowl in which you mixed the dough and place the dough back in the bowl. Cover and let stand in a warm place until doubled in size. Punch down dough and shape bread by pinching off the size desired. Fry in deep fat until brown on both sides.

The Chickasaw Festival, held at Tishomingo each year, honors the cultural heritage of the Chickasaw Nation.

Overnight French Toast

Elaine Levy   8 slices

8 slices French bread (¾ inch thick)
4 eggs
1 cup milk
2 tablespoons orange juice
1 tablespoon sugar
½ teaspoon vanilla extract
¼ teaspoon salt
butter
powdered sugar

- Arrange bread in a 9X12-inch baking dish.
- Mix eggs, milk, orange juice, sugar, vanilla extract and salt until well blended. Pour mixture over bread, turning bread to coat both sides. Cover and refrigerate overnight.
- Next morning, sauté bread in melted butter. Sprinkle with powdered sugar and serve with maple syrup.

Divine Cottage Cheese Pancakes

Eve Wegener   36 mini pancakes

1 cup cottage cheese, small curd
1 cup sour cream
4 eggs
¾ cup flour
1 tablespoon sugar

- Blend ingredients thoroughly in food processor or blender.
- Pour 3-inch pancakes on a lightly greased griddle and cook until cakes are golden brown on both sides.
- These are tender and delicious, especially with tart jam or jelly. May be made ahead. When ready to serve, layer with applesauce and heat in a 300 degree oven for 5 or 6 minutes. Dust with powdered sugar.

SOUPS & SALADS

SALADS

Fruit
Cranberry Salad,79
Cranberry Grape Salad,80
Frozen Fruit and Nut Medley,78
Ginger Ale Salad,80
Molded Ambrosia,81
Peach Melba Salad,79
Tropical Frozen Fruit Salad,78

Meat and Fish
Frosted Chicken Salad,84
Oh! That Salad by Committee!,77
Oriental Chicken Salad,83
Oriental Shrimp Salad,84
Raspberry Chicken Salad,82
Shrimp and Pasta Salad,82

Vegetable
Amish Cole Slaw,71
Blackeyed Pea Salad,72
Broccoli on the Cool Side,73
Caesar Salad,70
Calico Corn Salad,72
Cauliflower Salad,74
Herbed Green Pea Salad,73
Jazzy Zucchini Salad,74
Napa Cabbage Salad,71
Perle's Potato Salad,75

Potato Salad for a Crowd,76
Spaghetti Salad, 83
Spinach Salad,70
Tossed Salad for an Army,76
Zucchini and Basil Pasta Salad,81

SOUPS
Ado Annie's Curried Chicken Soup,64
Black Bean Soup,61
Brie Soup,57
Cold Strawberry Soup,56
Cream of Pumpkin Soup,58
Fresh Pumpkin Soup, 59
Gazpacho,55
Hearty Mennonite Soup,62
Jim Nabors' Alabama Chili,63
Lola's Clam Chowder,68
Neal's Chili,61.
Oven Chili,62
Posole,67
Quick Clam Chowder,68
Quick "Gourmet Tasting" Soups,69
Savory Onion Soup,60
Sopa de Helote (Corn Soup),60
Taco Soup,63
Tortilla Soup,66
Turkey Green Chile Soup,65
Venetian Soup,56
White Chili,65

THE CRYSTAL BRIDGE

Located in downtown Oklahoma City, the Crystal Bridge is an integral part of beautiful Myriad Gardens. Seventeen acres of trees and flowers encircle the conservatory, which bridges a downtown lake. A suspended skywalk provides opportunity for close communion with thousands of tropical and sub-tropical plants and an Adventure Trail winds through a 35-foot waterfall. The Gardens are the site for the annual Oklahoma City Arts Festival, now considered to be one of the top ten such festivals in the United States.

Gazpacho

Mary Helen Swanson   Makes 1 gallon.

3 to 4 fresh tomatoes, peeled and finely diced
2 to 4 medium cucumbers, peeled and finely diced
2 bunches green onions or 1 large bermuda onion, finely diced
2 medium green peppers, seeded and finely diced
3 stalks celery plus leaves, finely diced
1 can (42 to 46 ounce) tomato juice
1 bottle (32 ounce) Snappy Tom
¼ cup fresh lemon juice
1 tablespoon vegetable oil
2 teaspoons Crazy Salt (or Beau Monde seasoning)
1 teaspoon garlic salt
3 drops Tabasco

- Combine diced tomatoes, cucumbers, onion, green pepper and celery in a large mixing bowl and set aside. Except for the tomatoes, these may be diced in a food processor.

- Add remaining ingredients to vegetable mixture, stirring to mix well. In a blender, purée 5 cups of the gazpacho, then recombine with the remaining vegetable mixture. Refrigerate until thoroughly chilled, several hours or overnight.

- Serve ice cold in glass cups or bowls. Ice cubes may be added to each serving, along with croutons or a small dollop of sour cream garnished with a parsley sprig. Keeps for several days in the refrigerator or may be frozen.

Calories per serving: 42
Saturated Fat 0 g
Cholesterol 0 mg
Total Fat 1 g (14% of Calories)
Sodium 474 mg

Cold Strawberry Soup

Cold soup for a summer day!

Lou Pinkerton   4 servings

2 pints fresh strawberries, cleaned
1 ½ cups sugar
¾ cup sour cream
1 cup half and half
⅔ cup dry white wine

- Reserve 4 strawberries for garnish. Purée remaining berries with sugar in processor or blender. Strain through fine sieve into large bowl

- Whisk in sour cream, then half and half and wine.

- Serve in chilled cups, garnishing each with a strawberry and sprig of mint.

Variation: Fresh peaches may be substituted for strawberries.

Venetian Soup

Jack Harrold   6 servings

1 can (14 ½ ounce) chicken broth, refrigerated, fat removed and discarded
1 package (6 ounce) tortellini (cheese or meat)
½ teaspoon oregano
pinch rosemary
coarsely ground black pepper to taste
1 egg, beaten (optional)
green onion tops, chopped, for garnish
choice of cheese, shredded

- Bring broth to a boil. Add seasonings.

- Add tortellini and cook until tender and floating on top of liquid.

- Add egg to soup and pour into individual serving bowls.

- Garnish with chopped green onions and sprinkle with cheese.

Jack Harrold, a longtime visiting professor at the University of Oklahoma, shared this recipe, a favorite of Giovanni Martinelli (1885-1969), a world famous tenor.

Brie Soup

Linda Trippe   12 servings

4 shallots
2 garlic cloves
1 leek (use only white part)
¾ cup unsalted butter
¾ cup flour
4 cups fresh mushrooms, sliced
4 cups cream sherry
4 cups beef broth
½ pint heavy cream
salt, white pepper and leaf thyme
round of Brie

- Chop in a food processor or mince by hand the shallots, garlic and white part of the leek and sauté in the butter until soft.

- Add ¾ cup of flour and cook roux until blond in color. Add 4 cups of sliced mushrooms and mix gently. Set aside.

- In another saucepan, burn the alcohol from 4 cups of cream sherry.

- When there is no longer a flame, add beef broth and bring to a boil.

- Whisk hot mixture slowly into the mushroom roux. Add enough heavy cream to thin to the consistency you wish. Season to taste with salt, white pepper and a bit of leaf thyme.

- Pour over a wedge of the ripened Brie and serve immediately.

The Roosevelt Grill in Edmond was a favored Route 66 restaurant. This soup was a special feature on the menu. Reprinted from **Cooking with Harriette.**

Zucchini Soup

Becky Buchanan   8 servings

2 quarts chicken broth
1 onion, sliced
pinch of oregano
salt and pepper
4 to 5 zucchini, cut in chunks
1 can (16 ounce) early green peas

- Bring first four ingredients to a boil. Add zucchini and cook 30 minutes or until tender. Add canned peas. Mix in blender. Add dash of paprika.
- Serve hot or cold.

> Calories per serving: 92
> Saturated Fat 0 g
> Cholesterol 0 mg
> Total Fat 1 g (14% of Calories)
> Sodium 2025 mg

Cream of Pumpkin Soup

Mona Preuss   4 to 6 servings

½ cup onion, coarsely chopped
2 tablespoons butter
4 tablespoons flour
4 cups chicken broth
2 cans (16 ounce) pumpkin
1 teaspoon sugar
1 cup cream
salt to taste
pinch basil

- Sauté onions in butter until clear. Add flour and stir while cooking.
- Add chicken broth slowly while stirring.
- Add pumpkin and seasonings and mix well.
- Add cream last, heating thoroughly, but do not permit to boil.

Fresh Pumpkin Soup

Make a Thanksgiving splash!

Marge Duncan   6 to 8 servings

1 7 to 8 pound pumpkin
2 cups fresh bread crumbs
⅔ cups onion, finely chopped
6 tablespoons butter, divided
½ teaspoon salt
dash of pepper
½ teaspoon sage
dash of nutmeg
4 cans chicken stock
½ cup Swiss cheese, coarsely grated
1 bay leaf
½ cup heavy cream
1 tablespoon fresh parsley

- Preheat oven to 350 degrees.
- Cut the top from the pumpkin neatly so it may be replaced. Remove seeds and pulp.
- Press bread crumbs into the bottom of the pumpkin and place the pumpkin shell in a shallow baking dish. Place in the oven to dry for 15 minutes. Remove from oven and turn temperature up to 400 degrees.
- Sauté onion in 5 tablespoons of butter. Add salt, pepper, nutmeg and sage.
- Rub 1 tablespoon butter on inside of pumpkin, coating walls.
- Add onion and seasoning mixture to chicken stock. Stir in Swiss cheese and bay leaf. Add dried bread crumbs from pumpkin shell. Pour entire mixture into pumpkin and place top back on.
- Bake for 1 ½ hours. Turn oven to 350 degrees and continue to bake for 30 minutes longer. Remove from oven, remove bay leaf and stir in heavy cream. Top with parsley and serve from pumpkin immediately.

Hint: Scrape pumpkin from sides of shell when serving.

Savory Onion Soup

Fran Wise   8 servings

6 onions, sliced
4 tablespoons butter
½ cup white wine
3 to 4 cans (12 ounce) beef stock
salt and pepper to taste
Swiss Gruyère cheese

- Sauté onions in butter until tender.
- Add liquids and cook gently for approximately 30 minutes.
- Top with toasted and buttered slices of French bread and lots of Gruyère cheese.

Sopa de Helote (Corn Soup)

From South of the Border!

Señora Luis Herrera de la Fuente   4 to 6 servings

1 tablespoon butter
1 tablespoon flour
6 ears fresh corn (4 with firm kernels, 2 with tender kernels)
3 cups water
2 teaspoons Knorr chicken broth base
1 cup light sour cream

- Cut kernels off the corn cobs. Mix firm kernels in the blender with water.
- Force the mixture through a sieve or food mill. Place in pan and simmer until it thickens.
- In another pot, melt butter. Add flour and cook a few minutes while stirring. Add the corn mixture, the tender kernels of corn, the chicken broth base, salt and pepper to taste. Cook to boiling.
- Add sour cream just before serving.

Señor Herrera de la Fuente first conducted in Oklahoma City in 1971. He returned in 1978 as the permanent conductor after serving as Music Director of the Chile, the Peru and the Mexico National Orchestras. His conducting post in Oklahoma City extended through the celebrated 50th Anniversary year of the Oklahoma City Symphony, 1987.

Black Bean Soup

Pat Taliaferro   6 servings

1 package (12 ounce) black beans,
soaked overnight in water
10 cups water
1 large onion, chopped
1 pound lean ground beef
1 garlic clove, minced
1 teaspoon chili powder
2 teaspoons salt
½ teaspoon oregano
½ teaspoon cumin
1 bottle (4 ounce) taco sauce
1 can (4 ounce) chopped green
chiles
1 can (15 ounce) tomatoes and juice

- Rinse and drain beans. Add water and cook 2 to 3 hours until tender.
- Brown meat and onion. Drain. Add garlic, chili powder, salt, oregano, cumin, taco sauce, green chiles and tomatoes. Mix and add to beans. Simmer until seasonings are well blended.

Neal's Chili

Neal Carrick   8 to 10 servings

3 pounds chuck roast beef, cubed
⅜ inch
1 tablespoon vegetable oil
2 cans (14 ½ ounce) chicken broth
½ teaspoon oregano
2 tablespoons onion powder
1 tablespoon garlic powder
1 tablespoon paprika
4 teaspoons cumin
1 can (8 ounce) tomato sauce
½ to 1 tablespoon cayenne pepper
6 tablespoons chili powder

- Sear meat in oil. Add chicken broth and simmer covered one hour and 15 minutes, adding water if needed. Add other ingredients and cook another 45 minutes to one hour.

At the annual Stockyards Stampede in Oklahoma City, chili is served with a flair. Look for Neal, who is one of the stars.

Hearty Mennonite Soup

Jeannie Klaassen   8 servings

1 whole chicken OR
1 to 3 pound chuck roast or beef
ribs
4 medium potatoes, diced bite size
2 carrots, sliced
1 onion, finely chopped
1 small head cabbage, coarsely
shredded
1 small can tomato sauce
1 teaspoon salt, or more
several peppercorns
1 bay leaf
1 teaspoon dill weed
1 teaspoon parsley, or more
½ cup plain yogurt or sour cream

- If using beef, brown all sides then cover with water. Add seasonings (salt, etc.) and simmer for two or more hours. (If using chicken, omit browning, cover with water and simmer until tender.) Remove meat from broth, debone; cut meat into bite-size chunks and set aside.

- Cook potatoes, carrots and onions in broth while cutting up cabbage. Add cabbage and tomato sauce and as much of the meat as you like. Finally, add yogurt or sour cream.

Hint: The amount of broth used will make the soup as thick or thin as you like.

Borscht became part of the German Mennonite culinary heritage when Mennonites established farming settlements in Russia at Catherine the Great's invitation. This adaptation omits beets and is a hot, hearty soup.

Oven Chili

Wanda Cook   12 servings

3 pounds lean ground beef
2 medium onions, finely chopped
2 cans (15 ounce) diced tomatoes
2 tablespoons cumin
2 tablespoons chili powder
2 tablespoons brown sugar
2 cans Ranch Style chili beans
1 teaspoon salt
½ teaspoon pepper

- Preheat oven to 350 degrees.

- Sauté onions and meat together until pink is gone from meat. Drain away fat. Add tomatoes, spices, sugar and beans. Mix thoroughly. Salt and pepper to taste.

- Bake for 1 hour, stirring frequently. Do not cover.

Jim Nabors' Chili

Gomer's favorite chili!

Jim Nabors   4 to 6 servings

1 pound ground beef
2 tablespoons fat
1 teaspoon salt
2 to 3 tablespoons chili powder
1 can (8 ounce) tomato sauce
1 can (15 ounce) red kidney beans
1 medium onion, finely chopped
2 tablespoons vinegar
½ teaspoon garlic powder
1 can (15 ½ ounce) tomatoes

- Heat fat and quickly brown ground beef, stirring with a fork.
- Add remaining ingredients and mix well.
- Cover and simmer for 30 to 45 minutes, stirring occasionally.

> **"I**'ve always enjoyed chili and since leaving Alabama years ago, I have tasted every version you can think of. My favorite is still the one that my mother and sisters used back in Alabama. One of my fondest memories is sitting down to a dinner of chili and Southern style cornbread. So not only do I find this chili recipe my favorite, but eating it brings back loving memories of my childhood."

Taco Soup

Loretta O'Hara   10 servings

2 pounds lean, ground beef
1 small onion, chopped
3 cans (4 ounce) green chiles, chopped
1 teaspoon salt
1 teaspoon pepper
1 can (15 ounce) pinto beans, rinsed and drained
1 can (16 ounce) lima beans, rinsed and drained
1 package (1 ¼ ounce) taco seasoning
1 ½ cups water
1 package (1 ounce) ranch dressing mix
1 can (14 ½ ounce) stewed tomatoes
1 can (15 ounce) red kidney beans, rinsed and drained
shredded Cheddar cheese, optional
tortilla chips, optional

- In a large Dutch oven or kettle, brown beef and onion. Drain any fat.
- Add all remaining ingredients except cheese and chips. Bring to a boil.
- Reduce heat and simmer 30 minutes. Top with cheese and serve with chips, if desired.

Ado Annie's Curried Chicken Soup

Celeste Holm   10 servings

2 tablespoons butter
2 tablespoons extra virgin olive oil
1 medium onion, diced
2 large carrots, diced
3 celery stalks, diced
½ green pepper, diced
1 cup tomatoes (preferably Italian), chopped
1 large Granny Smith apple, chopped
1 ½ to 2 cups uncooked chicken, 1-inch cubes
⅓ cup flour
1 tablespoon curry
½ teaspoon ground nutmeg
pinch ground cloves
6 to 7 cups chicken stock/broth
1 ½ cups rice
⅓ cup currants
salt and pepper to taste

- Melt butter with olive oil in medium soup pot. Add onion, carrots, celery, green pepper; sauté 5 minutes.
- Add apple, tomato, chicken, and continue to sauté for 5 minutes.
- Mix flour with curry, nutmeg, and clove; add enough stock to make a watery paste. Add to pot and cook over low heat for five minutes.
- Add salt and pepper to taste.
- Add remaining stock, partially cover, and simmer for 35 to 40 minutes.
- Cook 1 ½ cups rice. Remove from heat and add ⅓ cup or more dried currants to top and replace cover.
- Add rice and currants to pot of soup and serve in warmed bowls or ladle soup over rice in individual bowls.

Celeste Holm, the original Ado Annie in the first production of the Broadway musical, **Oklahoma!**, graciously sent this recipe when she heard that **Applause** was a salute to the state of Oklahoma. As **Oklahoma** has played all over the world for the past 50 years, the spirit and the role of Ado Annie have become a part of American heritage and dear to the hearts of all Oklahomans near and far.

Turkey Green Chile Soup

Ava Wheaton   6 servings

6 cups low sodium chicken broth
2 chicken bouillon cubes (optional)
½ cup dry white wine
2 cups cooked turkey, cubed ½ inch
4 cups mixed vegetables, diced ½ inch (potatoes, carrots, onion)
1 can (4 ounce) chopped green chiles
1 ½ teaspoon oregano
1 ½ tablespoons cilantro, minced (or fresh parsley)
2 large garlic cloves, minced
cilantro or parsley for garnish

- Remove any fat from broth.
- In a 4-quart saucepan, bring broth, wine and minced garlic to boil and reduce to about 5 ½ cups of liquid.
- Reduce heat and add uncooked vegetables. Simmer until half cooked. Add turkey, chiles, cilantro or parsley, oregano and salt and pepper to taste. Continue to simmer until vegetables are well cooked and flavors well blended, about 20 to 30 minutes. Serve with jalapeño corn bread or hot tortillas.

Calories per serving: 182
Saturated Fat 1 g
Cholesterol 35 mg
Total Fat 4 g (18% of Calories)
Sodium 689 mg

White Chili

Katie Bates   8 servings

1 pound large white beans
4 cups chicken, cooked and diced
6 cups chicken broth
2 medium onions, chopped and divided
2 garlic cloves, minced
1 tablespoon oil
2 cans (4 ounce) chopped green chiles
2 teaspoon ground cumin
1 ½ teaspoon dried oregano
½ teaspoon cayenne pepper
1 block (8 ounce) Monterey Jack cheese, shredded

- Cover beans with cold water and soak overnight. Drain.
- Add chicken broth, half of the chopped onions and garlic to beans. Simmer 2 to 3 hours until tender.
- Sauté remaining onions with green chiles in oil until soft.
- Combine cumin, oregano, cayenne pepper and add to bean mixture. Add chicken and bring to boil and simmer 1 hour longer.
- Serve topped with Monterey Jack cheese.

65

Tortilla Soup

Barbara McCune   10 servings

4 tablespoons corn oil
4 corn tortillas, torn in large pieces
2 cloves elephant garlic, minced
1 ½ tablespoons epazote
1 cup onion purée
2 cups tomato purée
1 tablespoon cumin
2 teaspoons chili powder
3 bay leaves
8 cups chicken stock
dash cayenne pepper
4 chicken breasts, cooked and chopped
1 avocado, diced
1 cup Cheddar cheese, shredded
1 cup Monterey Jack cheese, shredded
6 corn tortillas, cut in strips and fried

- In a large stock pot, heat corn oil. Sauté epazote, garlic and torn tortillas briskly until soft. Add onion and tomato purée.

- Bring to a light boil. Add cumin, chili powder, bay leaves and chicken stock. Simmer and add salt and cayenne. Continue to cook for 45 minutes.

- Remove bay leaves. Purée mixture and return to heat for 20 minutes more.

- Place chicken, avocado, fried tortilla strips, and cheese in serving bowls. Pour soup mixture over and serve immediately.

Posole

Libby Britton

3 pounds pork loin roast
5 cups water
3 cups chicken broth
2 large onions, chopped
2 teaspoons salt
1 whole chicken
2 garlic cloves, crushed
4 teaspoons chili powder
½ teaspoon paprika
1 teaspoon cumin
1 teaspoon oregano
1 tablespoon bacon fat
2 cans (4 ounce) chopped green chiles
2 cans (16 ounce) white hominy, drained
garnishes: chopped onions, radishes, sliced avocado and lime wedges

- Place roast, water and broth in a large pot and heat to boiling. Add onions and salt. Reduce heat, cover and simmer for 30 minutes. Add chicken and heat to boiling. Reduce heat and simmer about 45 minutes. Remove pork and chicken from broth and cool. Cover and refrigerate broth.

- Cut meats into small pieces and refrigerate.

- Skim fat from broth. Stir garlic, chili powder, paprika, cumin and oregano into bacon fat over low heat. Stir in a small amount of broth and add mixture to rest of broth in the soup pot. Add hominy, heat to boiling. Reduce heat, cover and simmer 20 minutes. Add pork and chicken pieces and simmer 15 minutes longer.

- Serve in bowls and add garnishes as desired.

Hint: May substitute dried posole for hominy. Cover dried posole with water and soak overnight. Drain and add to mixture and cook until tender. This will need to cook longer than with hominy.

Quick Clam Chowder

Laura Pritchard   4 servings

3 slices bacon
½ cup onion, minced
1 can (6 ½ ounce) clams, save liquid
1 cup potatoes, cubed ¼ inch
1 can (10 ½ ounce) cream of celery soup
1 ½ cups milk
dash pepper

- Cook bacon in frying pan until crisp. Remove from pan, drain on paper towels and crumble into small pieces. Set aside.

- Brown onion in bacon fat. Add clam liquid and potatoes. Cover and cook over low heat until potatoes are tender.

- Blend in bacon, clams, soup and milk. Season to taste.

- Heat but do not boil.

Lola's Clam Chowder

Glenda Payne   4 to 6 servings

1 onion, chopped
¾ cup celery, chopped
2 tablespoons butter
1 bottle clam juice
3 cans (6 ½ ounce) clams, chopped, with liquid
3 to 4 potatoes, diced
½ teaspoon celery salt
½ teaspoon onion salt
2 tablespoons butter, melted
¾ cup half and half
2 tablespoons cornstarch
1 can (14 ounce) whole tomatoes
½ teaspoon pepper
fresh parsley, chopped

- Sauté onion and celery in butter until onion is translucent.

- In large pan, mix clam juice, clams and liquid. Add seasonings, sautéed vegetables and potatoes. Simmer, covered, until potatoes are soft, about 30 minutes.

- Melt butter. Add cornstarch and stir until well mixed. Add half and half and simmer until slightly thickened. Add tomatoes and pepper. Add to clam mixture, stir and heat but do not boil.

- Garnish each serving with parsley.

Quick "Gourmet Tasting" Soups

But don't tell anyone how you did it!

Ina Mae Schlegel   6 to 8 servings

CHICKEN CURRY SOUP

1 can (10 ½ ounce) cream of
chicken soup
1 can (10 ½ ounce) split pea with
ham soup
2 cans milk
salt, pepper and curry to taste

• Mix all ingredients. Heat well and serve.

CORN CHOWDER

1 can (16 ounce) yellow
creamed corn
2 cans (10 ½ ounce) cream of
potato soup
½ cup onion, chopped finely
3 cans (10 ½ ounce) milk
4 tablespoons butter
salt and pepper to taste

• Mix all ingredients. Heat well and serve.

TOMATO MUSHROOM BISQUE

1 can (10 ½ ounce) tomato soup
1 can (10 ½ ounce) cream of
mushroom soup
2 cups milk
2 tablespoons dry onion flakes
½ teaspoon garlic salt, or more
dash of cayenne pepper

• Empty the cans of soup into a saucepan. Stir the milk in gradually. Add the onion, garlic salt and cayenne. Heat well and serve.

Spinach Salad

Marge Duncan   8 servings

1 package washed spinach, torn in bite size pieces
2 hard-boiled eggs, chopped
½ pound bacon, fried crisp and crumbled
¾ cup garlic croutons

- Place spinach leaves in large bowl. Toss with Dijon dressing and garnish with eggs, bacon, and croutons.

DIJON DRESSING
2 teaspoons Dijon mustard
½ cup peanut or olive oil
⅛ teaspoon sugar
4 scallions, chopped
½ cup mayonnaise
¼ cup lemon juice
1 tablespoon tarragon vinegar

- Mix all dressing ingredients well. Pour over salad and serve.

Hint: You may top this with grilled chicken strips and serve it as an entrée.

Caesar Salad

Robert S. Kerr, Jr.   2 large servings

1 garlic clove
salt to taste
freshly ground black pepper to taste
4 to 6 anchovy filets
1 tablespoon white wine vinegar
2 tablespoons olive oil
½ teaspoon dry mustard
½ teaspoon Worcestershire sauce
1 lemon
3 to 4 cups Romaine lettuce, torn in bite-size pieces
1 egg yolk
½ cup fresh Parmesan cheese, grated
1 cup crisp toasted croutons

- Rub garlic around the inside of an unfinished wooden bowl with a fork until thoroughly mashed. Add salt and mash into garlic, then anchovy filets and mash until you have a smooth paste.
- Add vinegar, oil, dry mustard and Worcestershire to the bowl and mix thoroughly.
- Shake Romaine in a large towel to remove moisture, add to bowl and toss. Mixing well after each: squeeze lemon over salad; break egg yolk over all; and sprinkle with Parmesan cheese. Toss well, then add the croutons, salt and pepper to taste and serve immediately.

Amish Cole Slaw

Donita Phillips   10 servings

1 head cabbage, shredded
1 tablespoon salt
1 red bell pepper, chopped
1 green bell pepper, chopped
2 carrots, shredded
2 cups celery, chopped

DRESSING
1 to 1 ½ cups sugar
1 cup cider vinegar
1 to 1 ½ teaspoons celery seed
1 to 1 ½ teaspoons mustard seed

- Toss cabbage with salt and let stand 2 hours.
- Heat dressing ingredients; stir until sugar dissolves, about 10 minutes. Do not boil. Cool completely.
- Drain cabbage, add remaining vegetables and toss with dressing. Refrigerate at least 24 hours before serving. Lasts, refrigerated, indefinitely.

Calories per serving: 162

Saturated Fat 0 g	Cholesterol 0 mg
Total Fat 1 g (3% of Calories)	Sodium 932 mg

Napa Cabbage Salad

Mary Beebe Butts   8 servings

1 package Raman noodles, broken, uncooked
¼ cup margarine
4 ounces almonds, slivered
4 ounces sunflower hearts or sesame seeds
1 large Chinese (Napa) cabbage, shredded
6 green onions, sliced

- Brown noodles, almonds and sunflower seeds in margarine in a skillet. Remove and cool. Reserve.
- Mix and refrigerate cabbage and onions.
- Pour dressing over cabbage 15 minutes before serving. Mix well.
- Just before serving, toss in the noodle mixture, adding a crunchy texture.

DRESSING
½ cup tarragon vinegar
½ cup vegetable oil
⅔ cup sugar
2 tablespoons soy sauce

- Whisk these ingredients together until well blended.

Calico Corn Salad

Pat Hosty   12 to 15 servings

3 cans (16 ounce) white shoe peg corn, drained
1 can (8 ½ ounce) early green peas, drained
1 cup stuffed green olives, sliced
1 green pepper, chopped
1 large onion, chopped
2 ribs celery, chopped
2 tablespoons diced pimento
2 teaspoons basil, crushed
1 bottle (8 ounce) Italian salad dressing

- Mix all ingredients and marinate for 24 hours before serving. Keeps indefinitely when refrigerated.

Blackeyed Pea Salad

Betty Johnson   16 servings

4 packages (10 ounce) frozen blackeyed peas, thawed
1 bunch radishes, thinly sliced
2 bunches green onions, diced (tops included)
4 small jars marinated mushrooms
2 small jars marinated artichokes, quartered
2 small cans chopped green chiles
1 green pepper, diced
2 jars pimentos, chopped
½ cup parsley, chopped
2 cucumbers, diced
DRESSING
1 bottle (8 ounce) Italian salad dressing
2 tablespoons lemon juice

- Combine all of the salad ingredients.

- Combine dressing ingredients and pour over salad, mixing thoroughly.

Betty was principal bassoonist for 50 years in our orchestra. When New Year's Day arrives, Betty always prepares this salad to bring good luck to all her friends.

Broccoli on the Cool Side

Kristy Ehlers   12 servings

3 bunches fresh broccoli
1 cup cider vinegar
1 tablespoon dill weed
1 tablespoon Accent seasoning
1 teaspoon salt
1 teaspoon pepper
1 teaspoon garlic salt
1 ½ cups vegetable oil

- Cut broccoli into 2-inch pieces.
- Mix remaining ingredients, pour over, and chill.
- Drain a few hours before serving.

> Calories per serving: 70
> Saturated Fat 1 g
> Cholesterol 0 mg
> Total Fat 6 g (79% of Calories)
> Sodium 119 mg

Herbed Green Pea Salad

Cool and crunchy!

Susan Robinson   12 servings

4 packages (10 ounce) frozen green peas
1 cup celery, chopped
4 scallions, tops included, thinly sliced
½ cup vegetable oil
3 tablespoons white wine vinegar
1 tablespoon fresh basil, chopped
1 teaspoon sugar
1 teaspoon salt
¼ teaspoon freshly ground pepper
6 large lettuce leaves, rinsed and dried
1 large tomato, peeled and cut into wedges
3 tablespoons fresh parsley, minced
3 tablespoons fresh chives, minced

- Combine peas, celery and scallions in a large bowl, tossing lightly.
- In a small bowl, whisk together oil, vinegar, basil, sugar, salt and pepper. Pour over vegetables, stirring gently to coat. Cover and refrigerate 2 to 4 hours, no longer.
- To serve, arrange lettuce leaves on a large platter and spoon vegetables over. Arrange tomato wedges around salad and garnish with chives.

73

Jazzy Zucchini Salad
From an Oklahoma Mother of the Year

Christine Peters   10 servings

MARINADE
1 bottle (8 ounce) Italian dressing
1 envelope (1 ounce) buttermilk
dressing mix

5 small zucchini, thinly sliced
2 cans (15 ounce) ripe pitted olives
2 cans (15 ounce) artichoke hearts
1 large jar sliced mushrooms
2 cans (6 ounce) bamboo shoots
5 green onions, chopped (optional)

- Mix marinade ingredients. Set aside.
- Drain olives, artichoke hearts, mushrooms and bamboo shoots.
- Place vegetables in a large bowl. Add marinade, stirring well. Cover and refrigerate overnight.

Cauliflower Salad

Paula Apgar   10 servings

2 tablespoons butter, melted
1 cup bread crumbs
2 heads Romaine lettuce, torn
2 cups cauliflower florets

DRESSING
1 cup light mayonnaise
2 garlic cloves, minced
3 tablespoons lemon juice
2 tablespoons Parmesan cheese

- Brown bread crumbs in melted butter.
- Mix dressing ingredients and toss with lettuce. Place in large bowl. Cover with bread crumbs, then cauliflower. Cover with plastic wrap and refrigerate for at least 1 hour. Toss before serving.

Perle's Potato Salad

The Hostess with the Mostest!

Mary Jo Nelson   6 to 8 servings

6 medium-sized potatoes
4 bacon strips, minced
¼ cup onion, chopped
¼ cup celery, chopped
1 dill pickle, chopped

DRESSING
¼ cup water
½ cup vinegar
½ teaspoon sugar
½ teaspoon salt
⅛ teaspoon paprika
¼ teaspoon dry mustard

- Cook potatoes in their jackets in covered saucepan. Peel and slice while hot. Set aside.

- Sauté bacon. Add onion, celery and pickle. Continue cooking until brown.

- Combine all dressing ingredients and bring to a boil.

- Prepare dressing. Mix with vegetables and serve immediately. May be prepared ahead and reheated.

Oklahoma's Perle Skirvin Mesta probably was America's most famous and outstanding party hostess. Through the administrations of six presidents, Perle's parties made national headlines. Whether lavish or simple, the occasion was handled in excellent taste. This recipe, reprinted from her autobiography, was always served with steak to her favorite guest, Ike Eisenhower.

The parties in which she took most pride were those she staged in Luxembourg for thousands of American service men and women stationed in Europe after World War II. She never had fewer than several hundred guests. However, Perle Mesta's roots remained in Oklahoma.

The Skirvin Hotel, built by her father, stands as an excellent example of early twentieth century lavish hotel design. And her parents' home can still be found in Mesta Park, an area of Oklahoma City which has been revitalized and restored.

Those who have attended the musical, **Call Me Madam**, can appreciate this Oklahoman's vitality and zest for living... as a citizen of the world, but an Oklahoman at heart.

Tossed Salad for an Army

Symphony Showhouse Tea Room   100 servings

1 cup onions, minced
6 cups celery, diced
3 cups carrot, shredded
6 cups cucumbers, chopped
6 pounds tomatoes, cut in small
pieces
12 heads lettuce, torn
1 pound fresh spinach, torn
salt to taste
2 quarts dressing of your choice

- Mix all ingredients and toss just before serving. Add dressing and mix lightly.

Potato Salad for a Crowd

Symphony Showhouse Tea Room   80 servings

20 pounds red potatoes
3 bunches green onions, chopped
1 whole stalk celery, chopped
2 tablespoons basil, crushed
1 jar (22 ounce) sweet pickle relish
1 jar (8 ounce) Dijon mustard
1 jar (48 ounce) light mayonnaise
6 hard-boiled eggs, chopped

Calories per serving: 182
Saturated Fat 1 g
Cholesterol 20 mg
Total Fat 4 g (20% of Calories)
Sodium 227 mg

- Clean and quarter potatoes. Cover with water and bring to a boil. Cover and simmer until tender. Drain and cool. Slip skins from quarters and cut into bite-size pieces. Place in large mixing bowl. Add onions, celery, all other ingredients and toss to blend. Place in covered container and store in the refrigerator overnight before serving.

- To serve, line bowl with lettuce and spoon salad mixture into bowl. Sprinkle with paprika.

Oh! That Salad by Committee!

Everyone has his own part to play!

The Committee   36 servings

SALAD DRESSING BY COMMITTEE

1 cup vegetable oil
all the reserved artichoke juice
½ teaspoon garlic powder
½ teaspoon salad herbs
salt and pepper
⅓ cup wine vinegar
½ teaspoon dry mustard
1 teaspoon sugar

- Mix ingredients before meeting begins.

2 pounds baked ham, cut in chunks
2 pounds cooked chicken breast, chopped
1 pound cooked shrimp, halved
1 pound feta cheese, crumbled
1 pound Cheddar cheese, grated
1 dozen eggs, hard boiled and chopped
2 pounds crisp bacon, crumbled
2 bunches radishes, thinly sliced
4 avocados, chopped
2 bunches green onions, chopped
1 ½ pints cherry tomatoes, halved
1 can sliced black olives, drained
1 pound fresh mushrooms, sliced
6 assorted heads of lettuce, torn
1 bunch of fresh parsley, chopped
3 jars (6 ounce) marinated artichoke hearts, reserve juice

- Marinate the mushrooms and artichokes in the dressing prior to preparing the salad. You may do this at the beginning of your group's meeting.
- Just before you are ready to serve lunch, assemble all the ingredients, toss with the salad dressing and serve.

Hint: Assign each of your members an ingredient to bring. Pick up French bread and fruit. Voila! Lunch is ready!

Frozen Fruit and Nut Medley

Esther Bernstein   12 servings

1 package (3 ounce) cream cheese
3 tablespoons mayonnaise
½ cup maraschino cherries, halved
1 cup canned sweet cherries, halved
1 cup orange sections, cut in thirds
1 cup walnuts, chopped
1 cup crushed pineapple, drained
1 cup whipping cream

- Cream mayonnaise and cheese together. Combine cherries, orange sections, walnuts and pineapple with cheese mixture.

- Whip cream and fold into fruit mixture. Pour into 5-ounce custard cups.

- Place in freezer for approximately 3 hours. When frozen, remove from cups and serve on lettuce, watercress or endive.

Tropical Frozen Fruit Salad

Nancy King   18 servings

1 can (6 ounce) frozen orange juice
½ cup sugar
2 tablespoons lemon juice
1 can (20 ounce) crushed pineapple
1 can (16 ounce) apricot halves, cut into small pieces
6 large bananas, ½-inch chunks
paper baking cups

- Thaw orange juice but do not dilute. Add all other ingredients, including juices from canned fruits, and mix together well.

- Line muffin tins with fluted paper baking cups. Spoon mixture into cups and freeze.

> Calories per serving: 111
> Saturated Fat 0 g
> Cholesterol 0 mg
> Total Fat 0 g (0% of Calories)
> Sodium 2 mg

Peach Melba Salad

Symphony Showhouse Tea Room   100 servings

2 quarts whipping cream
3 teaspoons vanilla extract
2 packages (12 ounce) miniature
marshmallows
1 cup confectioner's sugar
100 canned peach halves

- Whip cream and add vanilla. Fold in marshmallows and sugar.
- Place 1 heaping tablespoon on each peach half. Serve in crisp lettuce cup.

Cranberry Salad

A Pecan Festival Winner!

Virgie Casselman   6 servings

1 package (3 ounce) raspberry
gelatin
1 cup boiling water
1 cup sugar
½ orange, peeled and chopped
½ apple, chopped
½ cup pecans, chopped
½ package cranberries, chopped

- Dissolve gelatin and sugar in boiling water. Refrigerate mixture until slightly thickened. Add fruit and nuts.
- Pour mixture into an oiled mold or glass casserole. Refrigerate several hours or overnight. Serve on crisp lettuce.

Calories per serving: 190
Saturated Fat 0 g
Cholesterol 0 mg
Total Fat 6 g (27% of Calories)
Sodium 1 mg

Ginger Ale Salad

Jeannette Sias   4 servings

1 package (3 ounce) lemon gelatin
1 cup hot water
1 cup ginger ale
¾ cup crushed pineapple, drained
½ cup fresh strawberries, sliced
1 cup fresh grapefruit sections, diced

- Dissolve gelatin in hot water, add ginger ale and chill until thickened.
- Fold in fruit and pour into individual molds. Chill until firm.
- Unmold on crisp lettuce.

Hint: Serve with whipped, fat free mayonnaise.

Calories per serving: 160	
Saturated Fat 0 g	Cholesterol 0 mg
Total Fat 0 g (1% of Calories)	Sodium 73 mg

Cranberry Grape Salad

Mona Preuss   12 servings

1 bag (12 ounce) fresh cranberries
1 ½ cups sugar
2 cups seedless red grapes
1 bag (8 ounce) miniature marshmallows
1 can (6 ounce) crushed pineapple, drained
½ cup nuts, chopped
1 ½ cups light whipped topping

- Pulse cranberries in food processor until chopped but not pulverized.
- Add sugar. Stir together and refrigerate for several hours.
- Drain through a sieve or colander until most liquid is removed (1 to 2 hours).
- Combine drained cranberries and remaining ingredients and chill.

Hint: You may substitute artificial sweetener for half of the sugar.

Molded Ambrosia

Symphony Showhouse Tea Room   90 servings

72 ounces orange gelatin
3 gallons reserved liquids from
fruits plus water to equal 3 gallons
6 cups pineapple chunks, reserve
liquid
6 cups mandarin orange sections,
reserve liquid
4 cups peach slices, reserve liquid
2 cups maraschino cherries,
quartered
8 bananas, diced
3 cups shredded coconut
assorted salad greens

- Dissolve gelatin in boiling water and fruit juices. Place in refrigerator until partially set.
- Add all the fruits and coconut. Mix and pour into pans. Chill until firm. Cut into squares.
- Serve on your favorite salad greens.

Zucchini and Basil Pasta Salad

June Parry   8 servings

4 medium zucchini
1 teaspoon salt
1 ½ cups fresh basil, chopped
½ cup olive oil
4 garlic cloves
¼ teaspoon dried oregano
6 cups chicken broth
¾ pound orzo
¼ cup lemon juice
¼ cup Parmesan cheese, grated
3 tablespoons parsley, chopped
salt and pepper

Hint: Orzo is a rice shaped pasta. Any small pasta may be used. May be served as a main dish or side dish with barbecued meats.

- Grate zucchini coarsely and place in a colander. Sprinkle with salt and toss. Let stand 30 minutes, stirring once or twice. Squeeze zucchini dry and transfer to a large bowl.
- Blend basil, oil, garlic and oregano together in food processor or blender. Add to zucchini.
- Bring chicken broth to a boil in a large pot. Add orzo and reduce heat, cooking until orzo is just tender, 9 to 12 minutes. Drain well.
- Stir pasta into zucchini. Add the lemon juice, grated cheese and parsley. Season to taste with salt and pepper.
- Serve warm, at room temperature, or chilled.

Shrimp and Pasta Salad

Sue Timberlake   8 servings

1 package (12 ounce) vermicelli
½ cup olive oil
2 cups small shrimp (or more)
½ cup French dressing
½ cup parsley, chopped
1 garlic clove, minced
1 cup celery, chopped
1 cup green pepper, chopped
1 cup scallions, chopped
"Jane's Crazy Salt" to taste

- Cook vermicelli according to directions, drain and mix with other ingredients.
- Refrigerate at least 2 hours before serving. Seasoning Salt may be substituted if you don't know "Crazy Jane!"

Raspberry Chicken Salad

Linda Coats   8 servings

8 smoked chicken breast halves
2 heads bibb lettuce
several kiwi, star fruit or apple pear
1 head radicchio
RASPBERRY DRESSING
¼ cup raspberry or wine vinegar
¼ cup olive oil
¼ cup water
½ red onion, chopped
minced garlic
salt and pepper
basil
½ cup raspberry preserves

- Slice the chicken and tear lettuce. Slice the fruit. Mix together.

- Mix salad dressing ingredients together and shake in a tightly covered jar.
- Add dressing to the salad just before serving.

> Calories per serving: 276
> Saturated Fat 1 g
> Cholesterol 68 mg
> Total Fat 8 g (28% of Calories)
> Sodium 238 mg

Oriental Chicken Salad

Carole Almond   4 to 6 servings

1 pound chicken breasts
½ cup sesame seeds
½ pound fresh bean sprouts
2 cups cabbage, shredded
4 large green onions, chopped

GINGER JUICE
3 tablespoons fresh ginger, peeled, chopped
5 tablespoons soy sauce
2 teaspoons white wine

GINGER SALAD DRESSING
1 teaspoon ginger juice
2 teaspoons dry mustard
½ cup soy sauce
3 tablespoons peanut oil
2 tablespoons rice wine vinegar
2 garlic cloves, minced
1 tablespoon sugar
2 teaspoons sesame oil
¼ cup green onions, chopped

- Cook chicken. Bone, skin and cut into small pieces.
- Toast sesame seeds in 350 degree oven for 5 minutes. Watch carefully to prevent burning.
- Blanch bean sprouts by placing in boiling water for 30 seconds. Drain.
- Combine all ingredients. Mix well.
- Combine all ginger juice ingredients in blender and mix until smooth.
- Combine all ginger salad dressing ingredients and mix well. Pour over chicken mixture and let stand 5 minutes. May be made 2 days ahead and refrigerated.

> Calories per serving: 343
> Saturated Fat 3 g
> Cholesterol 53 mg
> Total Fat 20 g (52% of Calories)
> Sodium 1763 mg

Spaghetti Salad

Barbara Peters   4 servings

1 package (8 ounce) spaghetti
½ cup sweet pickle juice
½ teaspoon salt
1 tablespoon poppy seed
½ teaspoon caraway seed
½ teaspoon garlic salt
1 teaspoon celery salt
2 stalks celery, diced
2 tablespoons parsley
1 bunch green onions, chopped

- Cook, rinse and drain spaghetti.
- Mix remaining ingredients and pour over the spaghetti.
- Chill and serve.

Oriental Shrimp Salad

Caroline Schieren   6 servings

1 bag (20 ounce) frozen green peas,
thawed and drained
1 can (8 ounce) shrimp or fresh
shrimp, chopped
1 cup celery, finely chopped
¾ cup mayonnaise
1 tablespoon fresh lemon juice
½ teaspoon curry powder
garlic salt to taste
½ cup unsalted cashews
1 can (5 ½ ounce) chow mein noodles
lettuce leaves for garnish

- Combine peas, shrimp, celery, mayonnaise, lemon juice, curry powder and garlic salt. Toss well. Cover and refrigerate at least 30 minutes.
- Add cashews and noodles and toss again. Serve on lettuce leaves.

Frosted Chicken Salad

Patsy Sinclair   6 servings

2 cups unpeeled red apples, diced
1 tablespoon lemon juice
4 cups chicken, cooked and diced
¾ cup mayonnaise
½ cup seedless green grapes, sliced
¼ teaspoon salt
⅛ teaspoon black pepper
1 ½ cups celery, chopped
lettuce leaves
sliced apples and grapes for
garnish
1 package (8 ounce) cream cheese
¼ cup mayonnaise

- Line a 1 ½-quart bowl with plastic wrap. Combine the first eight ingredients. Gently press mixture into the prepared bowl. Cover and chill several hours.
- Carefully unmold the salad onto a serving plate lined with a bed of the lettuce leaves.
- Combine the cream cheese and mayonnaise. Frost the salad. Garnish with apples and grapes. Chill for several hours.

Patsy has been a consistent winner with her wonderful recipes since the Watonga, Oklahoma Cheese Festival began. This pretty and tasty chicken salad won a blue ribbon.

VEGETABLES

V. VANN

VEGETABLES

All American Red Hot Black Beans,97
Asparagus Vinaigrette,87
Baked Onions,92
Candied Yam Boats,91
Chase Farm Cheese Grits,101
Corn Casserole,88
Eggplant Zucchini Ratatouille,89
Eggplant Pyramid,89
Fresh Tomato Pasta,101
Green Beans with Almonds,91
Maureen's Creamy Herbed Pasta,102
Mixed Bean Casserole,96
Outdoor Onions,90
Pasta Primavera,102

Perky Blackeyed Peas,99
Potato Latkes,90
Red Beans and Rice,98
Sauerkraut Supreme,88
Skillet Cabbage,87
Snappy Spaghetti Squash,94
Sour Cream Rice,100
Spinach Cups,93
Squash Soufflé,94
Stuffed Squash Mexicano,95
Three Pea Medley,98
Vegetable Melange,92
Wewoka Baked Beans,96
Wild Rice Bake,99
Wild Rice Pecan Pilaf,100

THE PIONEER WOMAN

The Pioneer Woman was commissioned by E. W. Marland, Oklahoma oilman and philanthropist. Created by Bryant Baker, a graduate of the Royal Academy of Art in London, this inspiring sculpture is now on the National Register of Historic Places. Featuring a pioneer woman with her son, the statue serves as a monument to the courage and dignity of women who helped settle the West in the last century. Located in Ponca City, the statue stands beside a museum, built of native stone, which contains relics and historiana of Oklahoma's pioneer women.

Asparagus Vinaigrette

Mary Frates   12 servings

48 large stalks of fresh asparagus
salted water

VINAIGRETTE
3 tablespoons white vinegar
½ teaspoon salt
1 teaspoon Dijon mustard
¾ cup walnut oil
1 tablespoon tarragon or parsley
fresh ground black pepper

> Calories per serving: 43
> Saturated Fat 0 g
> Cholesterol 0 mg
> Total Fat 3 g (60% of Calories)
> Sodium 26 mg

- Peel stalks of asparagus, cut off butts to make spears same length. Tie in bundles and boil in salted water slowly until just tender, 15 min. Plunge into cold water to save color. Drain and cool rapidly. When completely cold, arrange on tender greens on serving dish.

- Beat vinegar, salt, mustard and pepper. Then beat in oil and herbs.

- Pour sauce over asparagus 1 hour before serving. Turn once to thoroughly marinate.

Applause to Mary Frates, founder of the Oklahoma Summer Arts Institute at beautiful Quartz Mountain State Park, where students come from all over the country to study music, dance, visual arts, photography and writing.

Skillet Cabbage

Afaf Mahfouz   4 servings

4 cups cabbage, chopped
1 green pepper, chopped
2 cups celery, diced
2 large onions, sliced
2 tomatoes, chopped
¼ cup bacon drippings
2 teaspoons sugar
½ teaspoon salt
pepper to taste

- Combine all ingredients in a large skillet. Cover. Bring to a boil and cook 5 minutes over medium heat.

Hint: To cut down on fat content, you may use low-fat butter instead of bacon drippings.

> Calories per serving: 148
> Saturated Fat 4 g
> Cholesterol 9 mg
> Total Fat 10 g (59% of Calories)
> Sodium 234 mg

87

Corn Casserole

Ruth Dick   4 to 6 servings

1 can yellow cream corn
¾ cup yellow corn meal
6 tablespoons vegetable oil
2 cans (4 ounce) chopped green chiles
1 can whole kernel corn
½ teaspoon garlic salt
2 cups Cheddar cheese, shredded
1 small can pimentos, chopped

- Preheat oven to 350 degrees. Butter a shallow baking dish.
- Mix all ingredients. Pour into prepared dish and bake for 1 hour.

Sauerkraut Supreme

Bill Kamp   6 servings

1 quart sauerkraut
1 large white onion, chopped
12 ounces very lean smoked bacon, chopped
2 cups dry white wine
2 tablespoon brown sugar
1 tablespoon cornstarch

- Drain and rinse kraut.
- Sauté the chopped bacon and onion until onion is clear. Add the kraut to the pot and then the wine. Add enough water to cover the kraut about ¼ inch, or add more wine.
- Simmer covered over low heat for at least 5 hours, adding water when necessary.
- Add the brown sugar to kraut. Mix cornstarch in enough water to dissolve well and add to the kraut, cooking until thickened. Stir well and serve with Boots' Brats.

For four generations, the Kamp family grocery has served the Oklahoma City community. They are located in their original building which is now an Historical Landmark. After tasting Bill's recipe for Sauerkraut Supreme, you'll want it this way every time!

Eggplant Pyramid

Avis Scarramucci   4 servings

1 eggplant, peeled, ½-inch slices
1 large tomato, sliced thin
1 large onion, sliced thin
¾ cup butter, melted
½ teaspoon salt
½ cup Italian bread crumbs
½ teaspoon basil
¼ pound Mozzarella cheese
2 tablespoons Parmesan cheese, grated

- Preheat oven to 450 degrees.
- On a medium-size heat proof platter, arrange eggplant slices. Place a tomato slice and an onion slice on top of each eggplant portion.
- Drizzle with ¼ cup butter. Sprinkle with salt and basil. Cover and bake in oven for 30 minutes.
- Cut cheese in thirds, arrange on top of eggplant. Mix bread crumbs and remaining butter together. Sprinkle on top of casserole along with Parmesan cheese.
- Lower oven temperature to 375 degrees. Return to oven and bake uncovered 10 minutes.

Eggplant Zucchini Ratatouille

May be served hot or cold.

Afaf Mahfouz   6 servings

⅓ cup olive oil
2 garlic cloves, chopped
1 large onion, sliced in rings
2 zucchini, sliced and lightly floured
1 small eggplant, chopped
2 green peppers, cut in strips
4 tomatoes, peeled and sliced
salt and pepper to taste
1 tablespoon parsley, minced

- Sauté onion and garlic in oil until onion is soft. Add zucchini, eggplant and green peppers.
- Cover and simmer one hour. Add tomatoes and salt and pepper.
- Simmer uncovered till thick.
- Garnish with parsley. Top with grated Parmesan cheese, if desired.

Outdoor Onions

Jane Baker   Serves 4

4 sweet onions
½ cup butter
salt and pepper
8 fresh mushrooms, sliced
grated Parmesan cheese

- Quarter each onion, but do not cut all the way through. Spread the quarters apart on a square of aluminum foil. Dot each onion with 2 tablespoons of butter, 2 sliced mushrooms and salt and pepper to taste. Sprinkle with Parmesan.

- Wrap each onion in foil and place on the grill for 45 to 60 minutes, or bake at 350 degrees.

Potato Latkes

Traditional for Jewish Festival of Purim

Scott and Betty Gordon   4 to 6 servings

5 medium potatoes, peeled
1 small onion, peeled
1 teaspoon salt
¼ teaspoon pepper
2 tablespoons matzah meal
2 eggs
oil for frying

- Grate potatoes and onion in food processor.

- Place mixture in bowl. Add salt, pepper and matzah meal.

- In another bowl, beat eggs together. Add eggs to potato mixture and stir.

- Heat oil over medium heat. Drop spoonfuls of potato into oil and fry on each side until golden brown.

Hint: Serve with applesauce and sour cream.

Candied Yam Boats

Almeda Hamilton   6 servings

3 large yams
½ cup prepared mincemeat
2 teaspoons lemon juice
½ teaspoon salt
2 tablespoons butter, softened
¼ cup brown sugar
¼ cup pecans, chopped

- Preheat oven to 425 degrees.
- Scrub yams. Bake for 50 minutes or until soft. Reduce oven temperature to 350 degrees.
- Remove yams from oven and cut in half lengthwise. Carefully remove pulp from skins, leaving ¼-inch shell. Mash pulp, stir in mincemeat and lemon juice. Sprinkle shells lightly with salt and spoon pulp mixture into shells. Do not pack but mound evenly. If desired, bake in casserole dish rather than shells.
- Cut butter into brown sugar and salt. Stir in pecans. Sprinkle this mixture over filled potatoes. Bake uncovered at 350 degrees until heated through, about 20 minutes. May be prepared ahead and reheated.

Green Beans with Almonds

McAlester's Italian Festival   4 to 6 servings

2 tablespoons vegetable oil
1 onion, finely chopped
1 garlic clove, minced
1 pound fresh green beans, cooked
salt and pepper to taste
2 tablespoons slivered almonds
2 tablespoons Parmesan cheese, grated

- Heat oil in a skillet; add onion and garlic and sauté until golden brown. Add green beans and cook slowly until hot. Season with salt and pepper. Stir in almonds and sprinkle with cheese just before serving.

Hint: Mushrooms may be added for variety. And, you may substitute 1 teaspoon fresh basil, minced, for the Parmesan cheese.

91

Baked Onions

Susan Robinson   6 to 8 servings

4 large dry Spanish onions
2 cups beef stock
1 tablespoon butter, melted
1 teaspoon salt
2 teaspoons honey
¼ teaspoon lemon peel, grated
¼ teaspoon paprika
white pepper to taste
1 teaspoon thyme
2 bay leaves
¼ cup parsley, minced
TOPPING
2 tablespoons buttered bread crumbs
or finely chopped walnuts

- Preheat oven to 375 degrees.
- Peel onions, cut in half and arrange in large casserole. Combine remaining ingredients and pour mixture over onions.
- Cover and bake for 60 minutes or until onions are tender.

- Uncover and spoon bread crumbs or nuts over onions.
- Continue baking for 10 minutes more or until topping is crisp and brown.

Calories per serving: 116
Saturated Fat 1 g
Cholesterol 4 mg
Total Fat 4 g (27% of Calories)
Sodium 585 mg

Vegetable Melange

Afaf Mahfouz   6 to 8 servings

3 large tomatoes
2 tablespoons olive oil
1 green pepper, julienned
1 red pepper, julienned
1 large onion, sliced
4 ribs celery, sliced
¼ cup water
½ teaspoon basil, crushed
salt and pepper to taste

- Peel and cut tomatoes into wedges. Heat oil in large skillet over medium heat. Add green and red pepper, onion and celery. Stir and cook 2 or 3 minutes. Turn heat to low, add water, cover and cook 5 or 6 minutes longer, until vegetables are crisp tender. Add tomatoes and heat 1 or 2 minutes until tomatoes are heated through. Add basil, salt and pepper to taste.

Calories per serving: 76
Saturated Fat 1 g
Cholesterol 0 mg
Total Fat 4 g (49% of Calories)
Sodium 362 mg

Spinach Cups

Pam Woolbright   8 servings

½ cup butter, melted
12 slices white bread, crusts
removed
1 package (10 ounce) frozen
chopped spinach, thawed
2 eggs, beaten lightly
½ cup cream style cottage cheese
2 tablespoons Parmesan cheese,
grated
½ cup cream
½ teaspoon Worcestershire sauce
garlic salt to taste
pinch of sugar
paprika for garnish

- Melt the butter in a skillet. Cool. Coat both sides of bread slices with cooled butter. Press each slice into a muffin cup (or use a muffin tin).

- Squeeze as much water as possible out of spinach, using your hands. In a mixing bowl combine spinach and the remaining filling ingredients except paprika. Spoon about 2 tablespoons of filling into each bread cup. Sprinkle with paprika.

- Bake at 325 degrees for 25 to 30 minutes. Let cool a minute. Use a fork to lift out the baked spinach cups.

Snappy Spaghetti Squash

Mattie Perryman   Serves 2

**1 small spaghetti squash, cut
lengthwise in half, seeded
2 tablespoons butter
2 teaspoons ginger root, grated
1 teaspoon curry powder
salt and freshly ground white
pepper
1 teaspoon lemon juice
1 tablespoon cilantro, minced**

Calories per serving: 111
Saturated Fat 7 g
Cholesterol 31 mg
Total Fat 12 g (94% of Calories)
Sodium 706 mg

- Preheat oven to 400 degrees.
- Place squash, cut sides down, in shallow pan with 1 inch hot water. Bake 45 to 55 minutes or until tender. Remove from oven.
- Heat butter in large skillet. Add ginger root and cook over low heat 5 minutes. Stir in curry powder.
- Scrape squash flesh out of shell into skillet, breaking into strands. Simmer 5 minutes, tossing to coat with butter mixture. Season to taste with salt and pepper. Add lemon juice and cilantro and toss gently but well. Serve hot or tepid.

Squash Soufflé

Pat Hosty   4 servings

**2 pounds small yellow squash,
sliced
4 tablespoons onion, chopped
½ teaspoon salt
1 package (4 ounce) sharp Cheddar
cheese, shredded
½ cup cracker crumbs
¼ cup butter
paprika
salt and pepper to taste
2 eggs, beaten
¼ cup sour cream**

- Preheat oven to 350 degrees.
- Mix ½ teaspoon salt in water and bring to a boil. Add squash and cook until tender. Drain and cool.
- Mix eggs, ½ of the cheese, sour cream and squash in 1 ½-quart baking dish.
- Sprinkle with remaining cheese and cracker crumbs. Dot with butter and season with salt and pepper.
- Bake for 20 minutes and serve immediately.

Stuffed Squash Mexicano

Caroline Schieren   6 servings

3 medium-size yellow squash
2 garlic cloves, chopped
¼ cup onion, chopped
¼ cup green pepper, chopped
½ to 1 jalapeño, seeded and
chopped
1 tablespoon olive oil
1 teaspoon chili powder
¼ teaspoon salt
¼ teaspoon pepper
¾ cup Monterey Jack cheese,
shredded
3 tablespoons sour cream
2 tablespoons picante sauce
2 tablespoons Cheddar cheese,
shredded
1 tablespoon ripe olives, sliced

- Preheat oven to 350 degrees.
- Cook squash in boiling water to cover, 7 minutes or until tender. Drain and cool slightly. Remove and discard stems. Cut each squash in half lengthwise; scoop out pulp, leaving a ¼-inch shell. Reserve the pulp.
- Sauté garlic, onion, green pepper and jalapeño in olive oil until crisp tender. Stir in squash pulp and cook, stirring often, until liquid has been absorbed. Add chili powder, salt and pepper; remove from heat. Add Monterey Jack cheese and sour cream; stir mixture well.
- Place squash shells in a lightly greased 9x12-inch baking dish. Spoon squash mixture evenly into shells.
- Bake at 350 degrees for 25 minutes. Divide picante sauce, Cheddar cheese and ripe olives evenly among squash; bake an additional 5 minutes.

Mixed Bean Casserole

Jenny Montgomery   12 servings

1 pound bacon, fried but not crisp
2 tablespoons bacon grease
3 large onions, thinly sliced
¾ cup brown sugar
½ teaspoon garlic powder
½ cup vinegar
1 can butter beans, drained
1 can green beans, drained
1 can lima beans, drained
1 can kidney beans, drained
1 can baked or BBQ beans, not drained

- All cans of beans used in this recipe are 16-ounce size.
- Preheat oven to 350 degrees.
- Crumble ½ of the bacon.
- Cook onions, brown sugar, vinegar, and garlic powder in large skillet for two minutes using bacon grease. Add beans and crumbled bacon.
- Pour into a 9x13-inch pan. Top with bacon slices and bake 1 hour.

Wewoka Baked Beans

Leroy Orsburn   4 servings

2 cans (15 ounce) pinto beans
4 slices bacon
1 garlic clove, minced
¼ cup molasses
1 tablespoon Dijon mustard
¼ teaspoon pepper
1 cup onion, chopped
½ cup water
¼ cup ketchup
½ teaspoon ginger
½ teaspoon salt

- Preheat oven to 350 degrees.
- In a skillet, sauté bacon, onion and garlic for five minutes.
- Drain beans and combine with the onion mixture and remaining ingredients. Place in a one-quart casserole dish. Cover and bake 30 minutes. Uncover and bake an additional 30 minutes.

Each year hundreds of people arrive in Wewoka for the Oklahoma Sorghum Day Festival which revolves around a real old-fashioned sorghum mill. Leroy is well-known for his variety of recipes using sorghum or molasses.

All American Red Hot Black Beans

Bob Schmidt   6 servings

1 ½ cups dried black beans
1 splash cider vinegar
6 cups water
2 tablespoons vegetable oil
1 ½ onions, chopped, divided
1 red bell pepper, chopped
3 teaspoons salt, divided
¼ cup olive oil
3 garlic cloves, minced
1 cup tomatoes, peeled and chopped
3 jalapeño peppers, minced and seeded
2 tablespoons lemon juice
¼ teaspoon cinnamon
⅛ teaspoon ground cloves
½ teaspoon ground cumin (optional)
zest of two oranges
1 bunch cilantro, chopped

Calories per serving: 243
Saturated Fat 2 g
Cholesterol 0 mg
Total Fat 14 g (52% of Calories)
Sodium 1284 mg

- Rinse beans, place in a large pot and add water to cover. Add a splash of vinegar, bring to a boil, then remove from heat. Cover and allow to sit several hours or overnight.

- Drain and rinse beans and return to pot. Add 6 cups water, oil, half an onion and 2 teaspoons salt. Bring to a boil. Reduce heat, cover and simmer gently 1 ½ hours. Uncover and continue cooking until beans are completely tender.

- In a large skillet, heat olive oil and cook remaining onion with the garlic until soft. Add rest of ingredients except cilantro.

- Pour cooked beans and liquid into the skillet and stir. Cook on low 30 to 45 minutes, stirring often. Mixture should be thick, but still moist. Add water if needed. Add cilantro the last few minutes of cooking.

Red Beans and Rice

Yvette Fleckinger   10 to 12 servings

1 pound red kidney beans
2 yellow onions, chopped
4 garlic cloves, chopped
chunks of picnic ham or ham
hocks
salt and pepper to taste
2 bay leaves
cooked rice

- Soak beans in a large pot of water overnight if possible, but at least 1 or 2 hours. Drain.

- Cover beans in pot with fresh water and add onions, garlic and bay leaves. Cook 1 hour on low heat. Add the ham chunks. Continue cooking, adding salt and pepper to taste at the end. Serve over cooked rice.

Hint: If you like beans highly seasoned, cayenne pepper may be added for an additional spice. The secret to making good beans is to cook them on a slow fire in a covered pot for 4 or 5 hours.

Yvette, a League President, is a New Orleans native who really knows her red beans and rice. When she is cooking this dish, her kitchen smells just wonderful!

Three Pea Medley

Kay Lindsey   8 servings

1 package (10 ounce) frozen green
peas
1 package (10 ounce) frozen snow
peas
1 ½ cup sugar snap peas
3 tablespoons butter
2 tablespoons orange rind, grated

- Defrost frozen vegetables, blanch sugar snap peas. In a skillet, melt butter and sauté vegetables for 5 to 7 minutes. Stir in orange rind and serve.

Hint: If sugar snap peas are unavailable, increase the others by half and proceed.

Calories per serving: 96
Saturated Fat 3 g
Cholesterol 12 mg
Total Fat 5 g (43% of Calories)
Sodium 86 mg

Perky Blackeyed Peas

A New Year's Day favorite!

Betsy White   8 to 10 servings

2 large tomatoes, chopped
1 large onion, chopped
3 tablespoons butter
½ cup picante sauce
3 cans (16 ounce) blackeyed peas
½ pound smoked turkey sausage
or turkey ham
4 large garlic cloves, finely
chopped

- Sauté chopped onion in butter; add tomatoes and garlic and cook a few minutes longer.
- Add peas with liquid, picante sauce and meat. Bring to a boil and reduce heat. Simmer 15 minutes.

> Calories per serving: 198
> Saturated Fat 3 g
> Cholesterol 21 mg
> Total Fat 6 g (26% of Calories)
> Sodium 685 mg

Wild Rice Bake

Kathryn Steely   6 to 8 servings

1 cup wild rice
2 tablespoons butter
½ cup almonds, slivered
2 tablespoons chives, chopped
1 cup mushrooms, sliced &
sautéed
2 ribs celery, chopped
3 cups chicken broth

- Preheat oven to 325 degrees.
- Place rice in a sieve. Wash and drain under running water. Melt butter and add rice, almonds and chives. Cook and stir for 20 minutes over low heat. Almonds should be golden.
- Add remaining ingredients and pour mixture into a 1 ½-quart casserole dish. Heat broth to boiling and pour over rice mixture. Stir to mix well. Bake, covered, for 1 ½ hours or until liquid is absorbed.

99

Wild Rice Pecan Pilaf

Afaf Mahfouz   8 to 10 servings

4 cups chicken broth
1 cup wild rice, well rinsed
1 small package wheat pilaf
1 cup pecan halves
1 cup yellow raisins
1 bunch green onions, sliced thin
½ cup fresh Italian parsley, chopped
½ cup fresh mint leaves, chopped
zest of 2 oranges
2 tablespoons olive oil
1 tablespoon orange juice
freshly ground black pepper

- Bring broth to boil in medium pan. Add rice and return to boil. Reduce heat to medium low and cook, covered, for 50 minutes or until rice is tender. Do not over-cook. Remove to large bowl.

- In another pan, prepare wheat pilaf according to directions on package. Let cool 15 minutes before adding to rice. Add rest of ingredients and toss well. Serve warm.

Sour Cream Rice

Grace Boulton   6 to 8 servings

3 cups sour cream
2 cans (4 ounce) chopped green chiles
4 cups long grain rice, cooked
¾ pound Monterey Jack cheese, grated
½ cup sharp Cheddar cheese, grated

- Preheat oven to 350 degrees.

- Butter a 2-quart casserole. Mix sour cream and chiles. Place a layer of rice in the casserole dish, then a layer of sour cream and chiles, then a layer of Monterey Jack cheese (Swiss cheese may be substituted). Repeat. Bake for 20 minutes. Sprinkle sharp cheese over the top and continue baking 10 minutes longer.

Chase Farm Cheese Grits

With a Southwest flavor!

Jerry Love   8 servings

3 eggs, beaten
3 teaspoons salt
1 ½ teaspoons Tabasco
1 teaspoon paprika
6 cups boiling water
1 ½ cups quick cooking grits
1 pound Wisconsin cheese, grated
¾ cup butter

- Preheat oven to 350 degrees.
- Mix eggs, salt, Tabasco and paprika. Set aside.
- Add grits to water and cook according to package directions.
- Slowly add cheese, butter and egg mixture, stirring until well blended.
- Pour into a 2-quart casserole and bake for one hour, or until firm.

Fresh Tomato Pasta

Louise Berry   6 servings

12 ounces dried pasta
1 tablespoon olive oil
2 large garlic cloves
2 large tomatoes, fresh
1 cup basil leaves, fresh
salt and freshly ground pepper
1 tablespoon olive oil, plus extra
for drizzling
Parmesan cheese, freshly grated

- Cook pasta according to package directions. Meanwhile, pour 1 tablespoon olive oil into a serving bowl. Crush garlic cloves in a garlic press and drop pulp into oil. Stir. Set aside.
- Dice tomatoes and place into small mixing bowl. Chop basil leaves and add to tomatoes. Sprinkle with salt and pepper. Stir.
- Drain pasta thoroughly and place in bowl with garlic and olive oil. Drizzle a little more olive oil over pasta. Stir gently to coat.
- Add tomato mixture to pasta, toss gently, then season with additional salt and pepper, if desired. Sprinkle Parmesan cheese over pasta before serving.

101

Maureen's Creamy Herbed Pasta

Maureen McGovern   Serves 4 to 6

1 cup half and half
4 tablespoons butter
¼ teaspoon nutmeg, grated
1 pinch cayenne pepper
½ cup Parmesan cheese, freshly
grated
1 ½ cups mixed herbs (basil, mint,
watercress, Italian parsley and
chives), chopped
1 pound spaghetti, cooked al dente
Parmesan cheese and fresh herbs
for garnish

- In heavy saucepan, simmer half and half, butter, nutmeg and cayenne for about 25 minutes until sauce has reduced slightly and thickened.
- Whisk in Parmesan and fresh herbs and simmer another 10 minutes.
- Add cooked spaghetti and toss.
- Sprinkle with Parmesan cheese and fresh herbs before serving.

Pasta Primavera

Not for dieters, but so good!

Vince Bishop   6 to 8 servings

1 cup zucchini
1 cup yellow squash
1 cup broccoli
1 medium onion
2 garlic cloves
3 tablespoons butter
1 package (8 ounce) cream cheese
2 cups cream
1 cup milk
3 cups wide egg noodles
½ cup water
3 tablespoons cornstarch
2 teaspoons white pepper
2 teaspoons seasoned salt

- Chop zucchini, squash, broccoli and onion. Sauté vegetables and garlic in butter for about 4 minutes. Add cream cheese, melting completely.
- Add cream and milk and bring to a boil. Add pasta and cook over medium heat until noodles are done.
- Combine water and cornstarch and add to the vegetable noodle mixture.
- Cook 4 or 5 minutes.

Vince is chef at the Urban Market just down the mall from our Applause office. The Cookbook Committee watches with interest the unique menu selections which keep the patrons coming back each day. Terrific!

MAIN DISHES

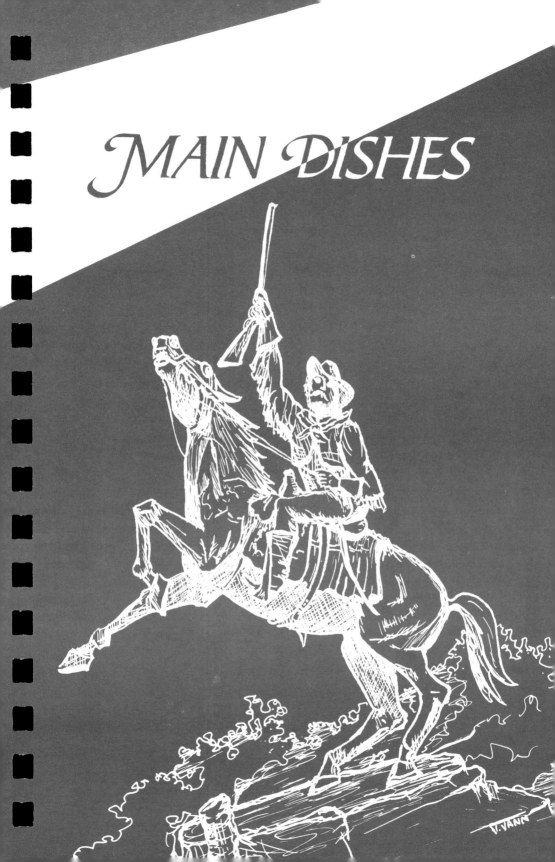

V. VANN

MAIN DISHES
BEEF
Barbeque Brisket,132
Beef Burgundy,137
Cajun Steak and Salsa,136
El Dorado Casserole,141
Herbed Steak with Red Pepper
Saffron Cream Sauce,134
Italian Pot Roast,131
Karen's Burgers,141
Mama Alessandro's Spaghetti and
Meatballs,140
Mexican Steak with Chile Cream
Sauce,135
Roast Tenderloin,130
Ropa Vieja (Old Clothes),139
Santa Fe Pot Roast,131
Short Ribs Carbonnade,133
Spanish Liver,139
Spicy Braccioli,137
Steak and Peppers,136
The Corner's Chicken Fried
Steak,138

EGGS AND CHEESE
Asparagus Quiche,164
Breakfast Soufflé,170
Cheddar Jack Cheese Pie,163
Homemade Egg Substitute,164
Low Fat Chile Rellenos
Casserole,166
Meatless Spinach Lasagna,167
Nancy's Deviled Egg Brunch,165
Oklahoma Brunch Casserole,163
Southwestern Omelet,169
Twenty Four Hour Omelet,168
Wine Eggs Mornay,165

FISH, SEAFOOD
Catfish
Catfish Kiev,124
Clams
Spaghetti with White Clam Chive
Sauce,129

Crab
Crab Cakes Orbach,119
Crab-Stuffed Eggplant,121
Marilyn's Crabmeat Bake,122
Orange Roughy
Orange Roughy Louie,125
Scallops
Coquilles St. Jacques Mornay,120
Salmon
Enrico's Salmon,122
Shrimp
Grilled Shrimp,125
Italian Baked Shrimp,127
Nanya Fried Shrimp,126
Shrimp Cheesecake,128
Shrimp and Pasta in Champagne
Sauce,127
Sole
Heavenly Sole,123
Swordfish
Smothers Brothers' Swordfish,124
Swordfish with a Flair,123
Tuna
Showhouse Tuna,129
GAME
Pheasant Normandie,158
Quail in Wine Sauce,159
Sherried Quail with Mushrooms,160
Warm Duck Salad,162
Wild Goose,161

LAMB
Grilled Rack of Lamb,154
Lamb Chops Teriyaki,155
Moussaka,153
Nettie's Leg of Lamb,154
Shepherd's Pie,157
Spring Lamb Stew,156

PORK
Boots' Brats,150
Brunch Bacon,149
Chalupas,147
Choctaw-Chickasaw Pashofa,151
Herbed Pork Tenderloin,145

Italian Festival Gnocchi,148
Mannheim Pork Roast,144
New Orleans Muffuletta
Sandwich,152
Old Fashioned Ham Loaf,150
Pasta and Prosciutto,149
Pork Chops with Apples,144
Pork Dijon,146
Pork Forestiori,145
Sausage and Mushroom Quiche,152
Savory Ham Slice,149
Spinach and Ham Torta,151

POULTRY
Cashew Chicken,111
Chicken Asparagus Casserole,109
Chicken Breast with Mushroom
Dijonnaise Sauce,113
Chicken Chili,116
Chicken Curry Casserole,108
Chicken Marengo,118
Chicken Mexicana,112
Chicken Pie Chilean Style,107
Chicken Puttanesca,114
Chicken Shrimp Supreme,110
Chicken Surprise,111
Chicken with Lime Butter,115
Light Lemon Chicken with
Thyme,117
Marilyn McCoo's Hot Chicken
Salad,112
Pecan Chicken,105
Southwestern Turkey Loaf,118
Tarragon Chicken Breasts,105
Teriyaki Chicken Wings,115
Tuscan Chicken with Yellow Pepper
Pasta,106
White Enchilada Casserole,108

VEAL
Itzhak Perlman's Favorite Veal
Loaf,142
Veal Marsala,143
Veal Paprika,143

THE NATIONAL COWBOY HALL OF FAME AND WESTERN HERITAGE CENTER

The 32-foot bronze statue of William F. "Buffalo Bill" Cody, on the grounds of the National Cowboy Hall of Fame in Oklahoma City, is a symbol of the Western spirit. Joel McCrea, in his movie role of Buffalo Bill, was the inspiration of sculpture by Leonard McMurray. Founded by Chester A. Reynolds in 1965, Western Heritage Center represents the seventeen Western states. Its purpose is to preserve accurately and authentically the rich heritage of the development of the Old West. The 37-acre site on Persimmon Hill was proclaimed a National Memorial by act of Congress in 1957. A $21 million expansion, completed in 1995, propels this outstanding museum into the 21st century.

Tarragon Chicken Breasts

Billie Hodgell   4 servings

4 chicken breast halves
⅓ cup light mayonnaise
2 tablespoons Dijon mustard
¼ cup milk
1 cup dry bread crumbs
2 teaspoons dry tarragon, crushed
salt and pepper to taste

> Calories per serving: 287
> Saturated Fat 2 g
> Cholesterol 77 mg
> Total Fat 7 g (24% of Calories)
> Sodium 850 mg

- Preheat oven to 350 degrees.

- Skin and bone chicken, removing all visible fat.

- Whisk mayonnaise, mustard and milk until well blended. Coat chicken with this mixture.

- Mix together bread crumbs, tarragon, salt and pepper. Dredge coated chicken in the crumb mixture. Place in a shallow pan that has been coated with vegetable spray. Bake, uncovered, for 45 minutes.

Pecan Chicken

A winning recipe from the Okmulgee Pecan Festival

Thelma V. Jordan   4 to 5 servings

½ cup biscuit mix
½ cup pecans, ground
1 teaspoon paprika
½ teaspoon salt
¼ teaspoon pepper
3 tablespoons butter
½ cup evaporated milk
1 2½ to 3 pound broiler fryer, skinned and cut up

- Preheat oven to 350 degrees.

- Combine and mix the dry ingredients. Set aside. Melt butter in a 13x9x2-inch baking dish. Dip chicken in milk, drain, then dredge chicken pieces in the pecan biscuit mixture. Place chicken in the prepared pan. Bake uncovered for 30 minutes. Turn chicken over, cover and bake an additional 30 minutes or until done.

Tuscan Chicken with Yellow Pepper Pasta

Mary Stuart   4 servings

2 tablespoons fresh sage, finely chopped
4 garlic cloves, minced
4 tablespoons olive oil
1 broiling chicken, quartered

- In a small bowl, combine sage, garlic and olive oil. Brush the chicken with the oil mixture. Let stand for an hour.
- Broil or grill over medium heat to desired doneness. Chicken should be golden brown.

YELLOW PEPPER PASTA
2 tablespoons butter
2 tablespoons olive oil
4 sweet yellow peppers, cut into strips
1 pound penne pasta, cooked al dente
salt to taste
½ cup Parmesan cheese, freshly grated
ground white pepper to taste

- Melt butter in a large skillet. Add the olive oil and pepper strips. Sauté peppers until soft. Add salt to taste.
- Pour pepper mixture into the bowl of a food processor fitted with a steel blade. Purée the peppers until very smooth. The peel should be completely processed.
- Pour the pepper purée over the cooked pasta and toss with Parmesan cheese. Add white pepper to taste.
- Serve broiled chicken and pasta with a green salad. Magnifico!

Mary brought this back to America from friends who have a vineyard between Siena and Florence. This is her favorite of all the Tuscany dishes she sampled.

Chicken Pie Chilean Style

"Rare Occasions"

Pat Bond   6 servings

2 tablespoons light butter
1 medium onion, chopped
1 garlic clove, minced
2 tablespoons flour, divided
2 cups low fat chicken broth, hot
½ teaspoon paprika
½ teaspoon ground cumin
½ teaspoon cayenne pepper
3 large tomatoes, peeled, seeded
and chopped
1 large green pepper, cut into
strips
1 large carrot, cut into thin rounds
3 cups cooked chicken, cubed
½ cup small pitted ripe olives
¼ cup sliced almonds
¼ cup raisins
1 can (16 ½ ounce) cream style corn
4 teaspoons sugar

- Preheat oven to 350 degrees.
- Melt the butter in a large skillet over medium heat. Add onion and garlic and sauté until soft. Blend in 1 tablespoon of the flour and cook, stirring, until bubbly. Gradually pour in the stock and continue cooking, stirring, until the sauce boils and thickens. Stir in the paprika, cumin, cayenne, tomatoes, green pepper, and carrot. Simmer for 5 minutes.
- Remove the pan from the heat and stir in the chicken, olives, almonds, and raisins. Pour the mixture into a shallow 2-quart casserole or an 11x9-inch baking dish.
- Wipe the skillet clean; heat the remaining 1 tablespoon flour and add the corn. Cook, stirring, until thickened. Spoon mixture over the top of the casserole, then sprinkle with the sugar.
- Bake for 35 minutes, then place under the broiler until the top is golden brown, about 5 minutes.

White Enchilada Casserole

Alan Valentine   8 servings

1 bag (16 ounce) tortilla chips
2 cans cream of chicken soup
1 pint sour cream
1 can (4 ounce) green chiles,
chopped
2 cans boned chicken (or 2 to 3
cups cooked)
1 large onion, chopped
1 package longhorn cheese (16
ounce), grated

- Preheat oven to 350 degrees.
- Mix together cream of chicken soup, sour cream, chiles, onion and chicken. In a 3-quart dish, layer chips, soup mixture and cheese, in that order, making two layers.
- Bake for 30 minutes at 350 degrees.

Alan Valentine is the Executive Director of the Oklahoma City Philharmonic Orchestra. His sound management has insured that the orchestra ends each season with a balanced budget. Oklahomans applaud him!

Chicken Curry Casserole

Nancy McGuire   6 servings

3 whole chicken breasts
20 fresh mushrooms
2 tablespoons butter
1 can (14 ounce) artichokes
⅓ cup wild rice, cooked in 1 can
chicken broth
2 cans (10 ½ ounce) cream of
mushroom soup
1 cup heavy cream
1 tablespoon curry powder
4 drops Tabasco sauce
4 tablespoons pimentos, chopped
6 tablespoons Parmesan cheese,
grated
paprika for garnish

- Preheat oven to 400 degrees.
- Cook chicken in salted water until tender. Bone and skin. Cut into cubes. Sauté mushrooms in butter, cut artichokes in half. Arrange chicken, artichoke hearts and mushrooms on bed of wild rice which has been cooked in chicken broth.
- Combine soup, cream, curry powder, and Tabasco. Heat, stirring constantly, until smooth. Add pimento.
- Pour mixture over casserole and sprinkle with cheese and paprika.
- Bake until bubbly, about 30 minutes.

Hint: Cream should cover chicken well and seep into the rice.

Chicken Asparagus Casserole

Florence N. Ratzlaff   4 servings

¼ cup butter
1 can (14 ½ ounce) asparagus spears
2 cups cooked chicken, chopped
1 cup Cheddar cheese, grated
1 package (8 ounce) corn muffin mix

- Preheat oven to 425 degrees. Melt butter in 8-inch baking pan.

- Drain asparagus, saving ½ cup liquid. Arrange spears in melted butter. Layer chicken and grated cheese.

- Prepare corn bread as package directs. Carefully spoon batter evenly on top of cheese layer.

- Bake for 20 minutes or until brown.

ASPARAGUS SAUCE
1 can cream of chicken soup
1 tablespoon lemon juice
½ cup green olives, sliced
½ cup liquid from canned asparagus

- Combine asparagus liquid with soup and lemon juice. Stir and heat. Add olives. Serve as sauce over top of each serving.

Chicken Shrimp Supreme

Dinner guests love this!

June Parry   15 servings

2 pounds small mushrooms
¼ cup butter
1 ½ tablespoons Worcestershire sauce
¾ cup sherry or dry white wine
5 chicken breasts, cooked, boned and cut into 2-inch pieces
3 pounds shrimp, cooked and peeled
3 cans (14 ounce) artichoke hearts, drained and quartered
½ cup Parmesan cheese, freshly grated

- Preheat oven to 375 degrees.
- Prepare White Sauce (see below).
- Sauté mushrooms in butter. Add Worcestershire sauce and wine and stir. Set aside.
- Place chicken, shrimp, artichokes and mushroom mixture in a greased three-quart casserole. Pour the White Sauce over the meats. Top with the cheese. Bake uncovered for 40 minutes or until bubbly.

WHITE SAUCE
⅔ cup butter
⅔ cup flour
4 cups milk
1 teaspoon salt
⅛ teaspoon nutmeg
¼ teaspoon pepper

- Melt butter in a saucepan over low heat. Stir in the flour and use a whisk to blend thoroughly. Add the milk and seasonings and cook, stirring, until the sauce is thick and smooth.

Recipe may be doubled for large crowds, but the sauce is best if two pans are used to cook the larger amount.

Cashew Chicken

Carol Sue Taylor   6 to 8 servings

8 chicken breasts
seasoned flour
shortening for browning chicken
1 can (13 ½ ounce) pineapple
chunks with juice
1 can (6 ounce) frozen lemonade,
thawed
1 medium green pepper, cut in
bite -size pieces
4 teaspoons brown sugar
1 teaspoon soy sauce
1 small package cashews

- Dredge chicken breasts in seasoned flour and brown in shortening. Drain on paper towels.
- In separate pan, heat remaining ingredients to boiling point.
- Return chicken to pan and pour ingredients over chicken. Cover the pan and simmer about 1 hour until very tender.

Chicken Surprise

A thousand dollar award winning recipe!

Debbie Ritter   6 to 8 servings

1 large spaghetti squash
1 block (8 ounce) mild Cheddar
cheese, shredded
1 block (8 ounce) Monterey Jack
cheese, shredded
1 large onion, diced
1 large can green chiles, diced
1 can cream of chicken soup
1 large can Milnot
3 chicken breasts, skinned, boned,
cut in ½-inch pieces

- Preheat oven to 350 degrees. Coat skillet with cooking spray.
- Sauté chicken pieces, covered, until done. Drain.
- Boil whole spaghetti squash, covered, approximately 20 minutes. Cut in half and scoop out "spaghetti".
- Mix soup and milk together. Layer in 9x13-inch pan using half of each: spaghetti squash, chicken, soup, onion, chiles and cheeses. Repeat process using remainder of each ingredient and ending with cheeses.
- Bake for 30 to 40 minutes, until cheese is bubbly but not brown. Serve immediately with crisp tortilla chips.

111

Chicken Mexicana

Joan Hambrick | 8 servings

8 chicken breasts, boned and skinned
2 tablespoons olive oil
1 can (15 ounce) tomato sauce
½ cup water
2 chicken broth cubes, dissolved
½ cup onion, chopped
1 can (4 ounce) diced green chiles
1 can (4 ½ ounce) black olives, chopped
2 tablespoons red wine vinegar
1 teaspoon ground cumin
½ teaspoon garlic salt
2 cups Monterey Jack cheese, grated

- Preheat oven to 350 degrees.
- Heat oil in a large skillet. Dredge chicken in flour and brown lightly on both sides. Drain on paper towels and place in a lightly buttered casserole.
- Mix the remaining ingredients, except cheese, in a saucepan and simmer five minutes. Pour over the chicken and cover tightly.
- Bake 45 to 60 minutes. Remove the cover, sprinkle with the cheese and bake 10 minutes more. Serve immediately.

Marilyn McCoo's Hot Chicken Salad

Marilyn McCoo | 6 to 8 servings

3 cups chicken, cooked and cubed
1 cup celery, chopped
¾ cup mayonnaise
¾ cup almonds, slivered and toasted
1 tablespoon lemon juice
1 tablespoon onion, chopped
2 tablespoons chicken flavored instant bouillon
½ cup potato chips, crushed
½ cup Cheddar cheese, shredded

- Preheat oven to 350 degrees.
- In a large bowl, combine all ingredients except chips and cheese. Mix well.
- Turn into 2-quart baking dish. Top with chips.
- Bake 30 minutes. Top with cheese. Bake 3 minutes longer or until cheese melts.

Marilyn is a top hit on the Pops Concert stage...and always plays to a full house in Oklahoma City.

Chicken Breast with Mushroom Dijonnaise Sauce

James Vallion   6 servings

6 boneless chicken breasts
⅔ cup vegetable oil
4 garlic cloves, minced
1 ½ cups of dry white wine

MUSHROOM DIJONNAISE SAUCE
2 cups fresh mushrooms, sliced and sautéed
2 cups heavy cream
4 teaspoons Dijon mustard
2 garlic cloves, minced
salt and pepper
fresh parsley, chopped

- Select nice boneless chicken breasts, remove skin and marinate in vegetable oil, fresh garlic and wine for 2 hours in the refrigerator.

- Afterwards, drain marinade, place chicken breasts in baking dish with small amount of white wine.

- Cook in 325 degree oven until firm. Remove from oven and keep warm.

- Place heavy cream, Dijon mustard and garlic in sauce pan and reduce by ⅓ over low heat.

- Add fresh sautéed mushrooms, salt and pepper to taste and place over the warm chicken breasts.

- Garnish with fresh chopped parsley and serve. You may double the servings by using one half breast per person.

This elegant dish of Master Chef, James Vallion, was served at a bi-annual Odyssey Gala, a major social event in Oklahoma City, which benefits the Oklahoma City Philharmonic. Jim's beautiful restaurant, The Eagle's Nest, is atop the United Founder's Life Tower. A panoramic view of the city, as the restaurant rotates, makes The Eagle's Nest one of the top dining attractions in central Oklahoma.

Chicken Puttanesca

Loretta Pickhardt   6 to 8 servings

3 tablespoons olive oil
8 chicken legs, drumstick and thigh, skinned, or chicken breast halves, boned and skinned
1 medium onion, thinly sliced
12 large garlic cloves, thinly sliced
2 cans (35 ounce) tomatoes, crushed
½ cup Nicoise olives (optional)
⅓ cup capers, drained
3 tablespoons sun-dried tomatoes, chopped
1 tablespoon mixed Italian herbs
1 tablespoon balsamic vinegar
pinch of red pepper flakes
salt and pepper to taste
Parmesan cheese, freshly grated

- Heat the oil in a large skillet. Add chicken and brown on all sides. Remove from pan and set aside.
- Add the onion and garlic to the oil and sauté until translucent. Stir in the crushed tomatoes and the remaining ingredients in order.
- Return the browned chicken to the pan and coat well with the sauce. Cover and simmer until chicken is tender, about 45 minutes.
- Serve over your favorite pasta sprinkled with lots of freshly grated Parmesan.

Oklahoma boasts two major symphony orchestras. Loretta is a former President of the outstanding Volunteer Council of the Tulsa Philharmonic.

Chicken with Lime Butter

Pam Woolbright   6 servings

**6 chicken breast halves, boneless
and skinless
salt and pepper to taste
⅓ cup vegetable oil
2 teaspoons fresh lime juice
8 tablespoons unsalted butter
½ teaspoon chives, minced
½ teaspoon dried dill weed**

- Sprinkle chicken breasts on both sides with salt and pepper. In a large skillet, heat oil to medium temperature. Add the chicken and sauté about 4 minutes or until lightly browned. Turn the chicken over and reduce heat to low. Cook 10 minutes or until done. Remove the chicken from the skillet and keep warm. Drain off remaining oil in the skillet and discard.

- To the same skillet, add the lime juice and cook over low heat until the juice begins to bubble. Add the butter, stirring just until the butter becomes opaque and forms a thickened sauce. Quickly stir in the chives and dill weed. Pour over the chicken and serve immediately.

Teriyaki Chicken Wings

Phyllis Stough   6 servings

**1 cup brown sugar, packed
1 cup soy sauce
1 cup sherry or dry white wine
3 large garlic cloves, minced
juice of 2 lemons
4 pounds chicken wings**

- Mix first 5 ingredients in a glass or plastic container. Add chicken. Cover and marinate in the refrigerator overnight.

- Next day, line a shallow baking pan with foil. Arrange the drained wings so they do not touch.

- Bake at 250 degrees for 2 hours, turning after 1 hour.

115

Chicken Chili

Libby Britton   6 to 8 servings

6 whole chicken breasts
6 tablespoons olive oil, divided
1 large onion, chopped
5 garlic cloves, minced
2 red bell peppers, diced
4 jalapeño peppers, seeded and
minced
3 tablespoons chili powder
1 ½ teaspoons ground cumin
1 teaspoon ground coriander
pinch of ground cinnamon
2 cans (16 ounce) tomatoes, puréed
1 cup black olives, sliced
1 cup beer
½ cup Worcestershire sauce
salt and pepper, to taste
cooked rice
Garnishes: sour cream, grated
Cheddar cheese, sliced green
onion, diced avocado

- Skin and bone chicken breasts. Cut meat into 1-inch cubes. Heat 3 tablespoons of the oil in a large pot. Add onion and garlic and sauté over medium heat 5 minutes. Add the peppers and sauté another 10 minutes. Stir in chili powder, cumin, coriander and cinnamon and cook 5 minutes longer, stirring constantly. Remove from heat and set aside.

- In a large skillet, heat the remaining 3 tablespoons of olive oil and brown the chicken in batches until just cooked through. Add the chicken to the large pot. Stir well and simmer 15 minutes over medium heat.

- Serve in deep bowls over cooked rice. Pass garnishes.

- May also be served with asodero cheese in a flour tortilla.

Light Lemon Chicken with Thyme

Carole Almond   4 servings

3 tablespoons flour
½ teaspoon salt
¼ teaspoon pepper
4 skinless, boneless chicken breast
halves
2 tablespoons olive oil
1 medium onion, chopped
1 tablespoon butter
1 cup chicken broth
3 tablespoons lemon juice, divided
½ teaspoon dried thyme
lemon wedges, optional
2 tablespoons parsley, chopped

Calories per serving: 263
Saturated Fat 3 g
Cholesterol 76 mg
Total Fat 12 g (40% of Calories)
Sodium 769 mg

- Mix flour, salt and pepper in a plastic bag. Dredge chicken in flour mixture. Reserve the excess seasoned flour.

- Heat the oil in a large skillet and brown the chicken about 5 minutes on each side. Remove the chicken to a plate.

- Melt the butter in the same skillet and add the onion. Cook until softened. Stir in reserved flour mixture.

- Add the broth, 2 tablespoons of the lemon juice and the thyme. Bring to a boil, stirring constantly. Return the chicken to the skillet, reduce the heat and cook on low, covered, about 5 minutes.

- Divide the chicken among the serving plates. Stir the remaining 1 tablespoon lemon juice into the sauce and pour over the chicken. Garnish with lemon wedges and parsley.

Chicken Marengo

Phyllis Olson — 6 servings

3 tablespoons flour
2 teaspoons salt
½ teaspoon pepper
2 2-pound chickens, disjointed
or
3 to 4 chicken breasts with bones
1 tablespoons olive oil
1 tablespoon cognac or brandy
2 garlic cloves, minced
1 celery rib, chopped
2 sprigs parsley
1 bay leaf
½ teaspoon dried thyme
2 tomatoes, peeled and diced
1 cup dry white wine
½ pound mushrooms, quartered
2 tablespoons parsley, chopped

- Mix flour, salt and pepper together. Lightly dredge chicken in flour mixture. Heat olive oil in skillet. Brown chicken then cool slightly. Heat the cognac and pour over chicken. Set it aflame. When flames die, add garlic, celery, parsley, bay leaf, thyme, tomatoes and wine.
- Cover and cook over low heat 30 minutes.
- Add the mushrooms and cook 15 minutes more or until chicken is tender. Taste for seasoning. Remove celery, parsley and bay leaf. Sprinkle with parsley and serve.

Calories per serving: 242
Saturated Fat 1 g
Cholesterol 68 mg
Total Fat 4 g (16% of Calories)
Sodium 1002 mg

Southwestern Turkey Loaf

Billie Hodgell — 6 to 8 servings

1 can (16 ounce) tomato sauce,
divided
1 pound ground turkey
1 egg
¾ cup tortilla chips, crushed
½ cup onion, chopped
¼ cup green pepper, diced
1 package taco seasoning mix
1 tablespoon Worcestershire sauce
1 teaspoon basil

- Preheat oven to 350 degrees.
- Reserve 1 cup tomato sauce. Mix remaining sauce with all other ingredients, except basil. Pack into a 9x5-inch loaf pan. Bake for 45 to 50 minutes.
- Heat reserved tomato sauce with basil and serve over the sliced loaf.

Crab Cakes Orbach

Harriette Orbach   4 servings

⅓ cup Roasted Garlic Mayonnaise
1 large egg white
¼ cup green onions, minced
2 tablespoons parsley, minced
1 tablespoon Dijon mustard
1 teaspoon Worcestershire sauce
½ teaspoon salt
½ teaspoon cayenne
1 pound lump crabmeat, picked over
½ cup fresh bread crumbs, divided
3 tablespoons unsalted butter, melted

ROASTED GARLIC MAYONNAISE
4 medium garlic cloves, unpeeled
1 large egg
1 tablespoon fresh lemon juice
salt and pepper
1 cup vegetable oil, olive oil, or a
combination of the two
2 tablespoons snipped fresh chives

- In a medium mixing bowl, whisk together the ⅓ cup of Garlic Mayonnaise, egg white, green onions, parsley, mustard, Worcestershire sauce, salt and cayenne. Add crabmeat and bread crumbs, stirring gently until just combined.

- With moistened hands form the mixture into 8 cakes. Coat each cake with remaining bread-crumbs. Chill the cakes on a plate, loosely covered, for 1 hour.

- Arrange the crab cakes on an oiled jelly roll pan, drizzle with half the butter and cook them under a preheated broiler, about 4 inches from the heat, for 4 minutes or until golden. Turn the cakes, drizzle with remaining butter and broil for 4 minutes more or until golden.

- Wrap the garlic cloves in a double thickness of foil and bake in a preheated 450 degree oven for 20 minutes. Cool and peel the garlic. In a food processor or blender combine the garlic, egg, lemon juice, salt and pepper. With the motor running add the oil in a stream and blend the mixture until it is just emulsified. Transfer the mayonnaise to a bowl and stir in the chives.

Coquilles St. Jacques Mornay

Memories of The Cellar in the Hightower Building!

Frank J. Hightower   4 servings

1 pound scallops
½ cup white wine
½ cup water
1 bay leaf
2 tablespoons butter
1 ½ teaspoons flour
¾ cup milk
2 tablespoons cream
5 tablespoons cheese (Swiss or Gruyére)
1 tablespoon bread crumbs
1 tablespoon parsley, chopped

- Simmer the scallops in wine, water and bay leaf gently for 5 minutes. Remove the scallops to a warm place and reduce the stock over high heat to about one tablespoon in quantity.

- In a separate pan, make a roux of butter and flour. Cook over low heat 5 minutes, occasionally stirring. Season.

- Remove from heat and stir in warm milk. Return to low heat and cook slowly, stirring, for about 10 minutes. Add one tablespoon reduced stock, cream and 4 tablespoons of the cheese. Simmer 5 minutes.

- Mix scallops into sauce and pour into shells or small baking dishes. Sprinkle tops with grated cheese, bread crumbs, and brown lightly and quickly under the broiler. Serve with a light sprinkle of parsley.

Crab Stuffed Eggplant

Michael Ashcraft   4 servings

2 eggplants
salt
4 tablespoons sesame oil
2 onions, finely chopped
1 tablespoon tomato paste
2 teaspoons paprika
½ teaspoon oregano
⅛ teaspoon cayenne
2 medium tomatoes, skinned,
seeded and cubed
1 pound uncooked snow crab,
shredded
½ cup Parmesan cheese, grated

- Trim the ends of the eggplants, cut into halves, and score the cut sides in a crisscross pattern. Salt and let stand 30 minutes.

- Rinse the eggplant and microwave 4 minutes on high, or bake in a hot (400 degree) oven for 15 minutes. Scoop out the centers and chop them.

- Heat the oil in a large frying pan and sauté the onions until soft. Add the tomato paste, paprika, oregano, cayenne and the chopped centers of the eggplants, mixing well. Add the tomato and heat thoroughly.

- Shred the snow crab carefully and add it to the tomato mixture.

- Stuff the eggplant halves with the mixture and top each with Parmesan cheese. Bake in a hot 400 degree oven for 15 minutes or until the crab is done.

Michael was Executive Chef at Les Caveaux, the first restaurant on the lower level at Maney House in Oklahoma City.

Marilyn's Crabmeat Bake

Marilyn Ehlers   10 to 12 servings

4 slices bread, diced
½ cup mayonnaise
1 green pepper, diced
1 onion, diced
1 cup celery, chopped
2 cups crabmeat, flaked
3 cups milk
4 eggs
4 slices bread, crusts removed
1 can cream of mushroom soup
1 cup Swiss cheese, grated

- Place diced bread in bottom of 9x13-inch baking dish.
- Mix mayonnaise, pepper, onion, celery and crabmeat and layer over bread cubes.
- Mix milk and eggs and pour over.
- Place slices of bread on top and refrigerate overnight.
- Bake at 325 degrees for 15 minutes. Remove from oven and pour mushroom soup over. Top with cheese and return to oven for one hour.

Enrico's Salmon

Sandra Flesher   2 servings

1 pound salmon
1 lemon, halved and divided
1 cup onion, finely chopped, divided
salt and pepper to taste
4 strips of bacon
1 ½ cups fresh spinach, finely chopped
¼ cup parsley, chopped
2 to 3 tablespoons mayonnaise
2 teaspoons vinegar

- Preheat oven to 350 degrees. Rinse salmon and pat dry. Place salmon on baking tray lined with foil. Rub salmon with lemon and with half of the onion. Salt and pepper as desired.
- Cover salmon with strips of bacon. Bake 10 minutes per pound. When cool, peel off bacon, skin and grayness and discard.
- Mix spinach, remaining onion and parsley. Add just enough mayonnaise, vinegar and lemon juice to make a thick sauce. Pour sauce over cooked salmon. Garnish with lemon wedges and parsley.

Sandy, oboist and English horn player with the Philharmonic, is a cherished member of the woodwind section. And you'll cherish her salmon recipe.

Heavenly Sole

Marge Duncan   6 servings

2 pounds skinless sole filets
2 tablespoons fresh lemon juice
½ cup Parmesan cheese, grated
3 tablespoons mayonnaise
¼ teaspoon salt
¼ cup butter, softened
3 tablespoons green onions, chopped
dash of Tabasco

- Place filets in a single layer on well greased bake-and-serve platter. Brush sole with lemon juice and let stand 10 minutes. Combine remaining ingredients and set aside.

- Broil the filets about 4 inches from the heat for 6 to 8 minutes. Remove from oven. Spread the cheese mixture over the sole. Broil 2 to 3 more minutes until lightly browned.

Swordfish with a Flair

Penny McCaleb   4 servings

2 tablespoons soy sauce
3 tablespoons fresh orange juice
1 tablespoon olive oil
2 tablespoons tomato paste
1 tablespoon fresh parsley leaves, minced
2 garlic cloves, minced
1 tablespoon fresh lemon juice
¼ teaspoon oregano
½ teaspoon black pepper, freshly ground
4 ¾-inch thick swordfish steaks

- In a bowl, whisk together the marinade ingredients. Place the swordfish in a shallow dish large enough to hold it in one layer. Pour the marinade over the fish. Cover and refrigerate for one hour, turning once.

- Remove the swordfish from the marinade and grill on an oiled rack over glowing coals for 4 to 5 minutes on each side.

Calories per serving: 167	
Saturated Fat 2 g	Cholesterol 53 mg
Total Fat 6 g (33% of Calories)	Sodium 226 mg

Smothers Brothers Swordfish

Tom and Dick Smothers   4 servings

4 1 to 1½-inch thick fresh swordfish
steaks
2 medium avocados, chopped in
small chunks
1 medium red onion, minced
6 sprigs cilantro, chopped
1 tablespoon fresh lemon juice
1 clove fresh garlic, minced
MARINADE
¼ cup soy sauce
2 teaspoons Worcestershire sauce
1 tablespoon lemon juice
¼ teaspoon garlic, mashed to a paste
salt to taste

- Cut a large pocket in each sword-fish steak with a sharp knife and set aside.
- Mix avocados, onion, cilantro, lemon juice and garlic in a bowl. Stuff mixture into the swordfish, securing with toothpicks if necessary.
- Pour marinade over the top, cover and refrigerate for several hours.
- Grill over hot coals, 2 to 4 minutes on each side, until done.

The Smothers Brothers delight Oklahoma audiences with their spirited banter. But the one thing they do agree upon...their swordfish recipe is healthy, delicious and great fun to grill outdoors.

Catfish Kiev

Rosalee Williams   6 servings

12 small catfish filets
1 teaspoon onion salt
1 package (3 ounce) cream cheese
with chives, softened
2 tablespoons butter, softened
1 teaspoon lemon pepper seasoning
1 can (4 ounce) mushroom stems
and pieces, drained and chopped
½ cup butter, melted
1 ⅓ cups seasoned crouton crumbs

- Preheat oven to 350 degrees.
- Sprinkle filets with onion salt. Combine the cream cheese, 2 tablespoons of butter and lemon pepper seasoning. Blend well. Stir in the mushrooms.
- Divide the cream cheese mixture into 12 portions. Roll each filet around a portion of the cheese mixture and secure with a wooden pick.
- Dip the fish into melted butter and coat with crumbs. Place the fish in a lightly oiled 9x13-inch baking dish. Drizzle with any remaining butter and bake 25 to 30 minutes.

Orange Roughy Louie

Another delicious entrée served at Odyssey!

James Vallion   2 servings

2 filets of orange roughy (5 to 8 ounce)
1 medium yellow onion, sliced
½ cup mushrooms, sliced
½ cup marinated artichoke hearts
½ cup dry white wine
pinch of tarragon

- Preheat oven to 350 degrees.
- Place filets in baking dish. Cover with onions, mushrooms and artichoke hearts. Pour wine over vegetables and fish. Top with a pinch of tarragon.
- Bake 18 to 20 minutes. Remove fish and vegetables to a serving dish. Reserve the cooking juices.

SAUCE
reserved cooking juices from baking fish
¼ cup lemon juice
1 teaspoon cornstarch
¼ cup water

- Pour cooking juices into a small saucepan. Add lemon juice and cornstarch which has been mixed with the water. Stir over low heat until thickened. Serve sauce over fish and vegetables.

Grilled Shrimp

Dee Dugan   6 servings

2 pounds large shrimp
1 garlic clove, minced
½ teaspoon salt
½ cup olive oil
¼ cup soy sauce
½ cup lemon juice
3 tablespoons parsley, chopped
2 tablespoons onion, finely minced
½ teaspoon pepper

- Shell and devein shrimp, leaving tails on if desired. Place in a shallow dish. Blend remaining ingredients in a dish and pour over the shrimp. Refrigerate, covered, 2 to 3 hours. If the shrimp are small, lace on skewers.
- Grill over flame at medium setting on a gas grill about 3 to 4 minutes on each side, until done. May be served as an appetizer.

Calories per serving: 189	
Saturated Fat 1 g	
Total Fat 6 g (30% of Calories)	Cholesterol 230 mg
	Sodium 401 mg

Nanya Fried Shrimp

Pexim (Phaik-Sim) Mui   4 servings

8 to 10 ounces rice vermicelli
8 ounces fresh shrimp, peeled,
deveined and sliced in half
lengthwise
4 tablespoons peanut oil
2 medium onions, thinly sliced
2 to 3 garlic cloves, minced
1 teaspoon lemon grass, finely
chopped
2 tablespoons light soy sauce,
divided
½ cup water, divided
2 teaspoons sugar
white pepper to taste
½ teaspoon salt
scallions to garnish, slivered

- Place vermicelli in a large bowl, cover with warm water and let soak for 5 to 7 minutes. Drain in a colander.

- Heat wok or frying pan on high heat, add peanut oil. When the oil is smoking, add the onions, lemon grass and garlic and stir fry for 2 to 3 minutes.

- Lower the heat to medium, add the shrimp and stir fry for 3 to 5 minutes or until the shrimp is just cooked.

- Mix the soy sauce, water and sugar and add half of this mixture and the vermicelli to the pan. Toss and stir until the sauce is absorbed.

- Add the remaining soy mixture, salt and pepper. Continue stirring until the liquid is almost all absorbed, taking care not to let the mixture stick in the base of the wok.

- Garnish with scallions and serve immediately.

Nanya style of food is an intriguing mixture of Chinese ingredients and Malay seasonings creating a blending of the two cultures.

Shrimp and Pasta in Champagne Sauce

Lu Garrison   6 servings

1 package (12 ounce) fettuccine
¼ cup butter
6 tablespoons green onion, chopped
1 ½ cups bottled clam juice
1 ½ cups heavy cream
1 ½ cups champagne
1 ½ pounds fresh shrimp, shelled and deveined
salt and pepper
chopped fresh parsley

- Cook fettuccine according to package directions.

- Meanwhile, melt the butter in a skillet over medium heat and sauté the onion until translucent. Add clam juice and boil until liquid is reduced by half. Add the cream, then shrimp and cook until the shrimp turns pink. Season to taste with salt and pepper.

- Drain the fettuccine, toss with the shrimp and sauce and sprinkle with parsley to serve.

Italian Baked Shrimp

Ellie Scherlag   8 servings

2 pounds shrimp, cooked and deveined
3 tablespoons olive oil
4 green onions, chopped
4 celery stalks, chopped
3 garlic cloves, crushed
1 green pepper, chopped
1 teaspoon fresh parsley, finely minced
1 teaspoon cornstarch
1 can (8 ounce) tomato sauce
½ teaspoon oregano
½ teaspoon basil
½ cup seasoned bread crumbs
1 cup mozzarella cheese, grated

- Preheat oven to 350 degrees.

- In a saucepan sauté onions, celery, green pepper, garlic and parsley in olive oil until soft. Stir in cornstarch until well blended. Add tomato sauce, oregano and basil and simmer for 15 minutes. Taste for seasonings.

- In a lightly greased casserole, layer shrimp and tomato sauce mixture. Top with cheese and bread crumbs. Bake for 30 minutes until bubbly. Serve with your favorite pasta.

Shrimp Cheesecake

Tish Eason   8 servings

1 ¼ cups club cracker crumbs
¼ cup butter, melted
1 ½ pounds fresh shrimp
2 tablespoons butter
⅔ cup green pepper, minced
¼ cup onion, minced
1 garlic clove, minced
2 packages (8 ounce) cream cheese
½ cup mayonnaise
4 eggs
⅓ cup milk
1 ¼ cups Swiss cheese, shredded
1 teaspoon white pepper

- Preheat oven to 300 degrees.
- Combine cracker crumbs and melted butter. Press into the bottom of a 9-inch springform pan.
- Peel, devein and chop shrimp. Melt the butter in a skillet and sauté the shrimp with the green pepper, onion and garlic for 4 to 5 minutes. Drain and set aside.
- Beat cream cheese and mayonnaise in electric mixer until light and fluffy. Add the eggs, one at a time, beating well after each. Reduce mixer speed to low and gradually add the milk. Stir in the shrimp mixture, Swiss cheese and pepper.
- Pour into the prepared pan and bake for 1 ½ hours, or until set. Turn off oven, open the door and leave cheesecake in the oven for 1 hour.
- Serve with Tomato Sauce.

TOMATO SAUCE
1 tablespoon olive oil
¼ cup onion, chopped
1 garlic clove, minced
2 cans (14 ounce) diced tomatoes, drained
½ teaspoon basil
½ teaspoon oregano
½ teaspoon marjoram
1 bay leaf

- Heat oil and sauté onion and garlic until onion is translucent. Add remaining ingredients and simmer, uncovered, about 20 minutes or until most of the liquid has evaporated. Stir occasionally. Remove bay leaf and serve warm over the cheesecake.

Hint: May be served in bite size pieces as an appetizer without the sauce.

Spaghetti with White Clam Chive Sauce

Ruth Ralston

4 servings

1 package (8 ounce) spinach pasta

- Prepare pasta according to package directions and drain.

CLAM SAUCE
2 cans (6 ½ ounce) minced clams (reserve liquid from one can)
1 package (6 ounce) cream cheese with chives
1 tablespoon chives or green onions, snipped
¼ teaspoon pepper
1 teaspoon Italian seasoning
1 garlic clove, minced
2 tablespoons olive oil
1 jar (2 ounce) pimientos, chopped and drained
1 can (4 ounce) mushrooms, drained
2 tablespoons ripe olives, quartered

- Combine all ingredients in a saucepan and cook on low heat for 20 minutes after cream cheese has melted. Serve over hot pasta.

Showhouse Tuna

Symphony Showhouse Tea Room

72 servings

36 cans (6 ounce) tuna
12 boiled eggs, chopped
1 whole stalk celery, chopped
2 jars (7 ½ ounce) sunflower kernels
2 jars (22 ounce) sweet pickle relish
3 cups salad dressing or mayonnaise

- Drain the tuna well. Add the rest of the ingredients and stir with a wooden paddle until all ingredients are well mixed. Add more mayonnaise if necessary for desired consistency.

Hint: Serve as a sandwich filling or use as a salad. Quarter a tomato, place on a lettuce leaf and fill with tuna mixture. This is easier if it is mixed in a large roasting pan!

Roast Tenderloin

Carol Williams   6 servings

CHEF'S SALT
1 cup salt
1 tablespoon Spanish paprika
1 teaspoon ground black pepper
¼ teaspoon ground white pepper
¼ teaspoon celery salt
¼ teaspoon garlic salt

- Mix well. One tablespoon of this mixture is to be used on the roast instead of salt. Store remainder for other purposes.

3 to 3 ½ pounds trimmed tenderloin
1 tablespoon Chef's Salt
1 teaspoon coarse black pepper
½ teaspoon sugar
2 tablespoons Kitchen Bouquet
¼ cup vegetable oil
1 cup red wine
½ cup vegetable oil

- Rub tenderloin with the sugar, Chef's Salt and pepper. Mix Kitchen Bouquet with ¼ cup oil. Pour over beef and rub into the roast. Let stand at room temperature.

- Preheat broiler. Line pan with aluminum foil. Place meat in pan and place as close to heat as possible. Turn often until surface is seared. Let cool at room temperature.

- Wrap meat in heavy aluminum foil. Pour wine over and close the top. Roast foil-wrapped meat at 350 degrees for 25 minutes. Remove, let stand at room temperature. May be kept for several hours.

Hint: Use the wine drained from meat for a sauce. Heat it with about 1 tablespoon arrowroot or enough to be of sauce consistency. This will be a pink juicy roast throughout.

- Half an hour before serving, heat ½ cup oil in small pan until it reaches the smoking point. Place unwrapped meat on cookie sheet covered with foil. Pour fat over meat and roast uncovered at 500 degrees for 10 to 15 minutes. Let it stand 10 minutes before slicing.

Santa Fe Pot Roast

Kudos for Oklahoma Cattlewomen, Inc.!

Russell King   10 servings

3 pounds lean, boneless beef chuck
roast
1 ½ teaspoons chili powder
1 teaspoon ground cumin
½ teaspoon garlic powder
¼ teaspoon black pepper
½ teaspoon dried oregano
1 tablespoon vegetable shortening
2 cans (14 ½ ounce) Mexican style
stewed tomatoes
1 can (4 ounce) chopped green chiles
½ cup ripe olives, drained and sliced
cilantro sprigs
sour cream

- Combine chili powder, cumin, garlic powder, pepper and oregano. Make small slits in the roast and insert some of the spice mixture.
- Place shortening in a Dutch oven over medium high heat. Brown roast on both sides. Add stewed tomatoes, chiles and olives. Cover and cook 2 hours or until tender.
- Remove roast to serving platter. Slice. Drain off excess liquid from tomato mixture and spoon it over the roast. Garnish with cilantro, if desired. Serve with sour cream.

Italian Pot Roast

Lynn Kickingbird   6 to 8 servings

¼ cup olive oil
3 pounds trimmed brisket or rump
roast
1 carrot, finely chopped
1 stalk celery, finely chopped
1 onion, finely chopped
2 garlic cloves, chopped
2 bay leaves
salt to taste
black pepper
1 cup red wine
1 can (6 ounce) tomato paste
1 can beef broth

Hint: You may double the quantity of meat, but you will only need to increase the sauce by one half. Brisket is usually best for this dish as it presents well.

- Preheat oven to 350 degrees. In a heavy Dutch oven, heat oil and brown the beef quickly on both sides. Remove beef from the pan and set aside.
- Sauté the vegetables in the Dutch oven until golden. Return the beef to the pan and add the rest of the ingredients. Bring mixture to a rapid simmer, stir gently, then cover and move to the heated oven. Bake 2 ½ to 3 hours. Meat should be tender and thoroughly cooked.
- Remove meat from pan and slice on the diagonal. Place on a serving platter. Skim fat from the gravy and discard. Serve the au jus either over the meat or in a gravy boat.

131

Barbeque Brisket
Ponca City's best!

Carey F. Head   25 servings

5 pounds beef brisket, trimmed
3 tablespoons Worcestershire
sauce
1 tablespoon Head Country
Seasoning
1 tablespoon liquid smoke
1 tablespoon vinegar
1 ½ cups Head Country Barbeque
Sauce

- Place brisket in pan lined with foil long enough to form a tent over the meat.

- Combine Worcestershire sauce, seasoning, liquid smoke and vinegar and marinate the brisket overnight, covered.

- Next day, bake at 275 degrees for five hours. Thirty minutes before the end of baking time, pour sauce over the meat. Continue to bake uncovered.

- Remove from oven and cool. Slice or shred, cutting against the grain. Serve with additional sauce, if desired. This will freeze and it reheats very well.

Although this brisket is best with the Head Country products developed by Tom Head right here in Oklahoma, you may substitute another low salt seasoning. Head Country Barbeque can now be made right in your own kitchen.

Short Ribs Carbonnade

Pam Woolbright   4 servings

2 pounds boneless beef short ribs
1 tablespoon butter
1 cup onion, thinly sliced
1 tablespoon sugar
1 bottle (12 ounce) beer
2 tablespoons vinegar
2 garlic cloves, minced
1 teaspoon dried parsley
salt and pepper to taste

- Preheat oven to 400 degrees. Place short ribs in casserole with butter, then place uncovered casserole in oven and brown ribs for 20 minutes on each side.

- Reduce oven to 350 degrees. Spread sliced onions over ribs. Mix remaining ingredients and pour over ribs. Liquid should come halfway up casserole sides. Add water if necessary.

- Cover tightly with foil. Bake 1 ½ to 2 hours or until very tender. Remove ribs to a serving platter. Transfer cooking liquid to a saucepan.

½ cup cold water
1 heaping tablespoon flour

- Shake flour and cold water vigorously until smooth.

- Add to pan juices in saucepan. Bring to a simmer over medium heat, stirring until smooth and slightly thickened.

133

Herbed Steak with Red Pepper Saffron Cream Sauce

Karen Davis   4 servings

4 choice ribeye steaks (8 to 10 ounces), 1 inch thick, trimmed
1 teaspoon coarse salt
2 teaspoons peppercorns, coarsely ground
2 teaspoons fresh thyme
1 teaspoon fresh rosemary
½ teaspoon garlic powder
3 tablespoons light olive oil

- Sprinkle both sides of the steaks with the salt and set aside for 10 minutes. On a large flat plate, mix the pepper, thyme, rosemary and garlic. Press both sides of the steak into the mixture. Distribute evenly among the four steaks.

- Heat 2 large, heavy skillets, preferably cast iron, over high heat. Add 1 ½ tablespoons of oil to each skillet. When the oil is almost smoking, add the steaks carefully. Immediately reduce the heat to moderate. Cook the first side until the bottom crust browns, about 4 minutes. Turn and finish cooking the steaks to the desired doneness. Serve on warm plates and pass the Cream Sauce.

RED PEPPER SAFFRON CREAM SAUCE
1 jar (8 ounce) diced pimientos, drained
½ cup cream
⅔ cup beef stock
½ teaspoon saffron threads
2 teaspoons lemon juice, or to taste
fresh rosemary or thyme sprigs for garnish

- In a small, heavy saucepan, combine the pimientos, cream, beef stock and saffron. Bring to a boil and reduce the mixture by half. Purée in a blender until smooth. Blend in the lemon juice. Keep warm until the steaks are ready.

Hint: To reduce calories, substitute nonfat sour cream for the cream in the sauce, adding it with the lemon juice.

The Oklahoma Beef Cook Off Festival awarded this elegant dish a blue ribbon.

Mexican Steak with Chile Cream Sauce

Jeannette Atwood   4 servings

---

4 sirloin steaks (6 ounce)
2 tablespoons chili powder
2 tablespoons vegetable oil
1 garlic clove, minced
¼ cup lime juice
1 tablespoon vegetable oil
1 can (15 ounce) yellow hominy with peppers
1 can (16 ounce) black beans

- Trim steaks, removing fat. Combine chili powder, vegetable oil, garlic and lime juice. Rub over steaks. Refrigerate at least one hour or overnight.

- Heat oil in heavy skillet over medium high heat. Add steaks and cook four minutes per side. Place steaks in center of large oven-proof platter.

- Drain and rinse black beans and hominy, combine and arrange around steaks. Cover with foil and place in 300 degree oven while you prepare the sauce.

CHILE CREAM SAUCE
1 can (4 ounces) green chiles, drained
⅓ cup whipping cream
⅓ cup sour cream
¼ teaspoon salt
2 tablespoons cilantro, chopped, optional

- Mash or purée green chiles. Combine with whipping cream in a small saucepan. Bring to boil.

- Reduce heat and simmer for 5 minutes. Whisk in sour cream, salt and cilantro. Serve sauce over the steaks or in a sauce boat.

Beef is king on the Oklahoma prairies. Jeannette's steak recipe was a prize winner at the Oklahoma Beef Cook Off. Your guests will applaud it as a prize winner, too.

Steak and Peppers

Sylvia M. Shirley   4 to 6 servings

1 ½ pounds round steak, tenderized
3 tablespoons vegetable oil
2 large green peppers, cut in 1-inch squares
3 onions, diced
1 ½ cups celery, sliced diagonally
1 ½ cups water
1 beef bouillon cube
2 teaspoons lemon juice
2 tablespoons soy sauce
2 tablespoons flour
½ teaspoon ginger
1 teaspoon garlic powder
steamed rice
crunchy Chinese noodles

- Cut the steak into finger-size thin strips.
- Heat oil in a large frying pan. Sauté beef until lightly browned. Add the vegetables and cook an additional 3 to 5 minutes.
- Mix the bouillon cube in the water. Add the lemon juice and soy sauce. Blend flour with the ginger and garlic powder and stir into sauce. Cook and stir until the sauce thickens.
- Serve over steamed rice and top with crunchy Chinese noodles.

Cajun Steak and Salsa

An Oklahoma Beef Cook-Off Winner!

Mary King   4 servings

SALSA
1 large tomato, seeded and chopped
¼ cup green onion, sliced
1 jalapeño pepper, seeded and finely chopped
¼ cup fresh cilantro, chopped
2 tablespoons fresh lime juice
1 teaspoon vegetable oil
¼ teaspoon salt
⅛ teaspoon cayenne pepper

CAJUN STEAK
4 beef eyes of round steak, 4 ounces each, ½ inch thick
½ teaspoon ground cumin
½ teaspoon cayenne pepper
½ teaspoon salt
2 teaspoons vegetable oil
⅓ cup sour cream, optional
cilantro sprigs for garnish

- Combine all salsa ingredients, mixing well. Set aside and refrigerate.
- Pat steaks dry. Combine cumin, cayenne pepper and salt. Rub steaks with these spices. Heat oil in a large heavy non-stick skillet over medium heat. Add steaks and cook 4 minutes or until desired doneness, turning once.
- Remove steaks to serving platter. Garnish steaks with salsa and cilantro sprigs. Serve with sour cream, if desired.

Spicy Braccioli

McAlester's Italian Festival   4 to 6 servings

8 sprigs parsley, chopped
1 garlic clove, minced
½ cup dry bread crumbs
1 tablespoon Parmesan cheese, grated
1 small onion, finely chopped
2 hard-cooked eggs, diced
2 strips bacon, diced
1 teaspoon salt
⅛ teaspoon black pepper
¼ teaspoon oregano
1 ½ pounds round steak, pounded on both sides
1 egg, beaten
2 tablespoons flour
¼ cup vegetable oil
¾ cup water
Bolognese Sauce, page 148 (optional)

- Preheat oven to 350 degrees. Place first ten ingredients in a bowl and mix thoroughly

- Lay the steak flat on a table. Spread mixed ingredients on top of the steak. Fold edges in and roll. Tie securely with string.

- Dip rolled and tied steak in the beaten egg, then in flour. Heat oil in a skillet. Sauté steak on all sides until golden brown. Place in a roasting pan. Add water and roast 45 minutes.

- Cut into 1 ½-inch slices and serve plain or with sauce over the steak.

Beef Burgundy

Laura Kerr Ogle   6 to 8 servings

3 medium onions, sliced
2 teaspoons butter
2 pounds lean beef, cut into 1 ½ x 1-inch strips
1 ½ tablespoons flour
salt and pepper to taste
½ cup beef bouillon
1 cup Burgundy wine
½ pound mushrooms, sliced

- Using Dutch oven, sauté onions in butter until translucent. Remove to a dish. Sauté meat in the same butter until browned. Sprinkle with flour, salt and pepper. Add the bouillon and wine, stirring well.

- Simmer 3 hours. The liquid seldom cooks away, but if it seems dry, add more bouillon and wine. Add the onions and mushrooms. Stir well. Simmer one hour longer. Serve over rice or noodles.

The Corner's Chicken Fried Steak.

Mary Evelyn Crabb   6 servings

2 eggs, well beaten
1 cup milk
1 ½ pounds round steak, cut ½ inch thick, tenderized
1 cup flour, seasoned with salt and pepper
4 tablespoons vegetable shortening

- Thoroughly beat together the eggs and milk. Set aside.
- Trim fat from the steak and cut into serving pieces. Heat the shortening in a cast iron skillet.
- Dip the steaks in the egg wash alternately with the flour four times. Fry until golden brown on both sides. If desired, cover with Milk Gravy. Serve immediately.

MILK GRAVY
2 tablespoons flour
skillet drippings
milk
salt and pepper to taste

- Add the flour to the hot drippings left in the skillet. Stir vigorously until blended and bubbly.
- Slowly add milk, stirring constantly, until the gravy is thickened to your desired consistency. Serve over the Chicken Fried Steak.

The Corner Restaurant in Edmond, just off Route 66, is purported to have originated chicken fried steak. This dish is a traditional favorite of native Southwesterners. It is always served with Milk Gravy and don't forget mashed potatoes.

Ropa Vieja (Old Clothes)

A traditional Cuban dish

Manuel Barrueco   6 to 8 servings

2 ½ pounds flank steak
2 bay leaves
¼ cup olive oil
1 large onion, thinly sliced
1 large green pepper, cut in strips
3 garlic cloves, finely chopped
2 cups tomatoes, chopped and drained
½ cup dry sherry
1 quart lightly salted water
salt and pepper to taste

- Place beef and one bay leaf in a large saucepan with salted water. Cook covered over low heat until meat is tender, 1 to 1 ½ hours.

- Remove meat and cool to room temperature. Cut into 2-inch chunks.

- In a large skillet heat oil over low heat. Cook onion, garlic and pepper until tender. Add tomatoes, sherry and remaining bay leaf. Cook uncovered 15 minutes.

- Shred meat with your fingers. Salt and pepper to taste. Add meat to tomato mixture and simmer 30 minutes. Remove bay leaves and serve with white rice. May be prepared a day or two in advance.

Spanish Liver

Mary Gordon Taft   4 servings

4 strips of bacon
1 onion, chopped
4 pieces calf liver
½ cup flour
1 teaspoon chili powder
1 can Niblets yellow corn
1 can (15 ounce) peeled tomatoes
½ teaspoon salt

- Preheat oven to 350 degrees. Fry the bacon until crisp and crumble. Leave about ⅓ cup of bacon grease in the pan and sauté the onion.

- Season the flour with chili powder and dredge the liver. Place liver in skillet and cover with the corn, tomatoes, salt and bacon. Simmer 20 to 30 minutes.

Mama Alessandro's Spaghetti and Meatballs

Betty Johnson   8 servings

MAMA'S RED SAUCE
1 medium onion, diced
1 tablespoon olive oil
1 can (6 ounce) tomato paste
1 can (8 ounce) tomato sauce
2 teaspoons sugar
1 teaspoon salt
¼ teaspoon oregano
2 cups water
½ cup parsley, chopped

- Brown onions in olive oil. Add tomato paste, sauce, sugar, salt, oregano , water and parsley.
- Simmer on low heat for twenty minutes. Set aside.

MEATBALLS
1 ½ pounds ground beef
½ pound ground pork
2 cups bread, crumbled
2 tablespoons Romano cheese, grated
2 eggs, beaten
olive oil
½ teaspoon ground cinnamon
dash ground cloves

- Mix meat, bread, cheese and then eggs. Form into 18 balls. Brown in olive oil over moderate flame, turning several times.
- Drop meatballs in sauce and let simmer slowly for 30 minutes.
- Add cinnamon and cloves, and simmer ½ hour longer
- Serve meatballs and sauce over spaghetti, cooked according to package directions.
- Garnish with additional Romano cheese.

Hint: Allow 4 ounces of uncooked spaghetti per person.

Victor Alessandro, conductor of the Oklahoma City Symphony from 1938 to 1951, brought world wide recognition to the state and the orchestra through weekly broadcasts of the orchestra over the Voice of America and the Armed Forces Network.

Karen's Burgers

Just right for feeding the little league team.

Karen Mayfield   8 servings

1 ½ **pounds ground beef**
1 ½ **teaspoon salt**
1 medium tomato, finely chopped
1 small cucumber, grated
1 small onion, finely chopped
⅓ **cup catsup**
⅓ **cup sweet pickle relish**
8 hamburger buns

- Lightly brown ground beef in large frying pan on grill at moderate temperature. Drain, sprinkle salt over meat. Add tomato, cucumber, onion, catsup, and relish and stir to combine.
- Cook, covered, 15 minutes. Serve on hamburger buns.

El Dorado Casserole

Amy Wineinger   10 servings

1 ½ **pounds ground beef**
½ **cup onion, chopped**
½ **teaspoon salt**
½ **teaspoon garlic, crushed**
2 cans (8 ounce) tomato sauce
1 cup black olives, sliced
1 container (12 ounce) cottage cheese, small curd
1 cup sour cream
1 can (4 ounce) chopped green chiles
1 package (8 ounce) Monterey Jack cheese, grated
1 bag (16 ounce) tortilla chips, crushed

- Preheat oven to 350 degrees. Brown ground beef with onion, salt and garlic. Add tomato sauce and olives and simmer for 15 minutes.
- In a bowl, combine cottage cheese, sour cream and chiles.
- Place half of the crushed chips in the bottom of an ungreased 9x13-inch baking pan. Add a layer of meat, cottage cheese, sour cream and chile mixture, and a layer of cheese. Repeat with remaining half, ending with chips.
- Bake for 35 minutes or until bubbly. Casserole may be made the night before and refrigerated. Adjust the baking time to 45 minutes.

Itzhak Perlman's Favorite Veal Loaf

Itzhak Perlman   10 servings

4 small onions, chopped
1 garlic clove, minced
4 ½ pounds ground veal
2 eggs
ketchup to taste
pepper to taste
garlic salt to taste
1 to 2 cups boiling water
8 ounces bread crumbs, flavored

- Sauté onions until translucent, adding garlic toward the end.
- Place the meat in a large bowl, adding the onion, ketchup, pepper and salt. Knead by hand. Add the water, bread crumbs and eggs. Mix well by hand.
- Shape into 2 loaves in baking tins and bake 30 to 40 minutes in a preheated 350 degree oven. "Stick a knife in. If it comes out cold, it's not ready; if it's warm, it's time to eat."

Oklahoma City has applauded Perlman from the first time he came here as a very young man. He is truly the "King of the Violin".

Veal Marsala

Pat Taliaferro   6 servings

2 pounds veal, cut into thin slices
½ cup fresh Parmesan cheese,
grated
½ cup butter, divided
1 cup fresh mushrooms, finely
sliced
¼ cup beef stock
1 tablespoon flour
1 teaspoon beef extract
⅓ cup Marsala or sherry
parsley, chopped
freshly ground pepper

- Dip the veal slices in the grated cheese. Sauté the mushrooms for 1 minute in half the butter. Using a slotted spoon, remove the mushrooms from pan and reserve. Add flour to the pan and blend in. Add beef stock and extract to pan and stir over medium heat for about 1 minute. Add wine and cook another 10 seconds.

- In another pan, melt the remaining butter and sauté the veal slices about 1 minute. Add the veal and mushrooms to the sauce and heat. Arrange on a warm platter. Sprinkle with parsley and pepper and serve.

Veal Paprika

Susan Robinson   6 servings

2 pounds boneless veal stew meat
¼ cup butter
½ cup onions, minced
½ cup water
4 teaspoons beef stock base
2 cups dry white wine
1 teaspoon salt
½ teaspoon Mei Yen seasoning
¼ teaspoon thyme
1 tablespoon paprika
1 teaspoon lemon peel
½ cup sour cream
2 tablespoons sherry

- Wipe meat with damp cloth. Brown slowly in butter. When meat is browned, add onions and cook 5 minutes.

- Dissolve beef stock base in hot water and pour over veal. Add wine, salt, and Mei Yen. Crush thyme and stir into veal along with paprika and lemon peel. Cover and cook over low heat for 1 ½ to 2 hours or until meat is tender.

- Just before serving, stir in sour cream. Heat thoroughly but do not boil. Add sherry and serve at once.

Mannheim Pork Roast

A Mannheim Steamroller's Hit!

Chip Davis   8 to 10 servings

1 loin of pork, about 4 pounds
salt to taste
½ teaspoon thyme
½ teaspoon rosemary

- Preheat oven to 450 degrees.
- Place the roast, fat side facing up, on a rack in a shallow open pan. Sprinkle lightly with salt, pepper, thyme and rosemary.
- Roast 1 ¾ to 2 hours or until the internal temperature is 160 degrees. For easier carving, let roast rest about 10 minutes.

After working the Goodwill Games in St. Petersburg, Russia, Chip Davis took time away from his Mannheim Steamrollers to send this delicious and easy recipe.

Pork Chops with Apples

Jacquelyn Stengel   8 servings

8 pork chops
½ teaspoon salt
½ teaspoon thyme
4 apples
¼ cup brown sugar
2 tablespoons flour
1 cup hot water
1 tablespoon apple cider vinegar
½ cup white raisins

- Preheat oven to 350 degrees. Spray skillet with vegetable cooking spray. Brown chops and sprinkle with salt and thyme. Place chops in a casserole dish.
- Core and slice apples and layer over the chops. Sprinkle sugar over the apples.
- Add flour to skillet in which chops were browned. If there is no fat in the pan add one tablespoon vegetable oil. Stir flour constantly until browned but not burned. Add water and vinegar and cook until thickened. Add raisins and pour mixture over chops. Cover and bake for one hour.

Pork Forestiori

Jean Fishburne   4 servings

2 ½ pounds pork tenderloin
Dijon mustard
cracked pepper

- Coat tenderloin with mustard, then with cracked pepper. Place on broiler rack and broil on center rack of oven for 20 minutes.
- Remove pork from oven and slice into ½-inch thick slices. Return to oven and broil 1 to 2 minutes longer. Serve topped with Forestiori Sauce.

FORESTIORI SAUCE
4 slices bacon,
½ cup onion, diced
¼ cup parsley, chopped
4 cups mushrooms, sliced
2 garlic cloves, crushed
¼ teaspoon Worcestershire sauce
½ cup dry sherry
¼ cup brandy
½ cup beef broth
¼ cup whipping cream

- Cut bacon into 1-inch pieces and fry in skillet until brown. Remove bacon and pour off all but one tablespoon of the fat. Return the pan to medium heat and sauté onion, parsley and mushroom until the onion is translucent. Add garlic, Worcestershire, sherry, brandy and broth. Reduce heat and simmer 10 to 15 minutes. Immediately before serving, stir in cream. Pour the warm sauce over sliced pork to serve.

Herbed Pork Tenderloin

Jan Bowles   8 servings

⅓ cup olive oil
2 garlic cloves, minced
2 teaspoons rosemary leaves, crushed
2 teaspoons thyme, crushed
½ teaspoon salt
¼ teaspoon pepper
2 pork tenderloins
2 ½ pounds new potatoes, quartered

- Preheat oven to 375 degrees.
- Combine olive oil, garlic, rosemary, thyme, salt and pepper. Coat the tenderloins with 3 tablespoons of this herbal mixture and place in a large roasting pan.
- Toss the quartered potatoes in the remaining herbal mixture, and arrange around the meat.
- Roast 35 to 40 minutes, or until 155 degrees and juices run clear.
- Stir pot once, and broil on top rack 5 minutes to brown. Let stand 5 minutes, slice and serve.

145

Pork Dijon

Joanna Todd | 6 servings

4 to 5 pounds pork tenderloin
½ cup dry vermouth
½ cup sherry
4 to 8 ounces Dijon mustard, to taste
2 medium onions, peeled and sliced
cooking spray

- Preheat oven to 325 degrees.

- Spray a frying pan with cooking spray and sauté the onions until translucent. Transfer the onions to a casserole dish and set aside.

- Remove any membrane and fat from the pork and discard. Cut the meat into 4-inch lengths and brown in the frying pan. Transfer the pieces to the casserole.

- Pour the wines into the frying pan to deglaze. Add generous amount of mustard. Pour the mustard mixture into the casserole. Cover and bake for 90 minutes. Serve over noodles, accompanied with a steamed green vegetable and hot, crusty French bread.

Calories per serving: 278
Saturated Fat 4 g
Cholesterol 83 mg
Total Fat 12 g (38% of Calories)
Sodium 197 mg

Chalupas

Diann Lemons   6 to 8 servings

2 pound pork roast
1 package (16 ounce) pinto beans
2 garlic cloves
2 tablespoons chili powder
1 tablespoon ground cumin
1 teaspoon oregano
1 tablespoon picante sauce
2 teaspoons salt

- Place pork roast in a crock pot or large stock pot for cooking on the stove top. Add pinto beans and cover with water. Stir in the other ingredients. Cover and cook for eight hours on low heat on the stove, or for 12 hours on high in the crock pot.

- Stir meat mixture to blend. Serve over crushed corn chips or Chickasaw Fry Bread with shredded lettuce, shredded cheese, chopped onions, chopped tomatoes, sour cream and chopped olives. Top with picante sauce as desired.

Italian Festival Gnocchi

A touch of Little Italy!

McAlester's Italian Festival   6 servings

6 large potatoes, unpeeled
2 eggs, beaten
2 tablespoons oil or butter
1 teaspoon salt
½ cup Parmesan cheese
1 to 1 ½ cups flour

- Boil potatoes in their jackets until tender. Peel. Mash or put through a potato ricer. Blend in eggs, oil, salt and cheese. Then add flour, a little at a time, until all is blended together. Knead dough lightly on a floured board and form into little ropes, 1 inch in diameter. Cut each rope into pieces ¾ inch long. Cook in salted, boiling water until gnocchi rise to top of water. Cook a little longer, 2 to 3 minutes. Drain. Serve with Garlic Butter or Bolognese Sauce.

BOLOGNESE TOMATO SAUCE
¼ cup oil
1 onion, diced
¼ pound salt pork, diced
½ pound hot or mild sausages, sliced
½ pound beef, cubed
salt to taste
2 garlic cloves, minced
1 teaspoon basil
¼ teaspoon pepper
1 teaspoon dried parsley
1 bay leaf
1 can (29 ounce) tomatoes, crushed
1 can (6 ounce) tomato paste
1 can (6 ounce) water
½ cup dry white wine
1 can (4 ounce) mushrooms, undrained

- Heat oil in a saucepan. Add onion and salt pork and sauté until onion is golden brown. Add sausages and beef and brown slowly. Add salt, garlic, basil, pepper, parsley, bay leaf, tomatoes, tomato paste and water. Stir well. Add wine and mushrooms. Cook slowly for 2 hours. Serve over gnocchi or any pasta of your choice.

GARLIC BUTTER
1 garlic clove, mashed
1 cup butter, melted
salt, pepper and oregano to taste
grated Parmesan cheese

- Add salt, pepper, oregano and garlic powder to butter. Pour over gnocchi and toss lightly. Spoon onto a serving platter and sprinkle with cheese. Serve hot.

Brunch Bacon

Dare to be different!

Feodora Steward   4 servings

**2 egg yolks
1 teaspoon dry mustard
3 tablespoons Worcestershire
sauce
16 bacon slices, cut in half
fine cracker crumbs**

- Preheat oven to 325 degrees.
- Beat yolks, mustard and Worcestershire sauce together. Dip bacon in mixture, then roll in cracker crumbs. Place on a rack in a shallow pan and bake 15 to 20 minutes until bacon is browned and crisp.

Savory Ham Slice

Dorothy Dinsmoor   4 servings

**1 one-inch ham slice
½ cup orange marmalade
½ cup dry vermouth
1 teaspoon Kitchen Bouquet
½ teaspoon dry mustard
½ teaspoon ground ginger**

- Preheat oven to 350 degrees.
- Place the ham slice in a shallow baking dish. Combine remaining ingredients and spread over the ham.
- Bake for 45 minutes.

Pasta and Prosciutto

Lorraine Lear   6 servings

**1 package (8 ounce) linguine
1 package (10 ounce) frozen
asparagus
2 tablespoons butter, melted
½ cup Parmesan cheese, grated
½ cup plain yogurt
½ cup dry white wine
1 package (6 ounce) prosciutto, cut
into 1-inch strips
additional Parmesan cheese**

- Cook pasta and asparagus according to package directions.
- Combine butter, cheese, yogurt and wine. Stir in asparagus and prosciutto.
- Toss cheese mixture with drained pasta. Sprinkle with additional Parmesan cheese before serving.

Boots' Brats

Boots Taliaferro   4 servings

8 bratwurst sausages
1 ½ cups beer

- Marinate the brats overnight in the beer. Reserve the beer for the sauce.

SAUCE
1 ½ tablespoons vegetable oil
reserved beer
2 large onions, coarsely chopped
2 tablespoons dark brown sugar
2 tablespoons cider vinegar
1 bay leaf
1 tablespoon paprika
½ teaspoon salt

- Combine all sauce ingredients and mix well. Cook on medium heat for 5 minutes to reduce liquid. Refrigerate overnight.
- When ready to serve, grill brats 6 to 8 inches above the charcoal, 7 minutes per side or until nicely browned. Baste with sauce the last 2 minutes of grilling time. Serve with Sauerkraut Supreme.

Old Fashioned Ham Loaf

Nancy Apgar   6 servings

1 ½ pounds lean smoked ham, ground
½ pound veal (½ pound lean pork may be substituted)
2 eggs
1 cup tomato juice
¾ cup cracker crumbs
½ teaspoon dry mustard
¼ teaspoon black pepper

- Preheat oven to 400 degrees.
- Combine ingredients. Use loaf pan, firmly patting ingredients to achieve a rounded, dome top to the loaf.
- Bake 15 minutes at 400 degrees. Lower heat to 325 degrees and bake an additional 1 ¼ hours, basting several times with the sauce.

BASTING SAUCE
½ cup vinegar
2 tablespoons brown sugar

- Mix vinegar and brown sugar and use for basting ham loaf.

Spinach and Ham Torta

Pam Woolbright   4 servings

1 pastry for 9 to 9 ½-inch pie
1 cup onion, finely chopped
2 tablespoons olive oil
1 package (10 ounce) frozen chopped spinach, thawed and squeezed dry
½ cup Parmesan cheese, shredded
½ cup ricotta cheese
2 eggs, lightly beaten
½ cup half and half
1 cup smoked ham, diced or sweet Italian sausage, cooked and crumbled
¼ teaspoon ground sage
½ teaspoon salt
freshly ground black pepper, to taste

- Preheat oven to 425 degrees.
- Sauté onions in olive oil until tender and translucent. In a mixing bowl, combine the onions and thawed spinach. Stir in the cheeses, eggs, cream, ham, sage, salt and pepper.
- Position the pastry in a pie dish or tart pan. Gently press the dough against the sides of the pan and flute the edges. Add the filling. Bake about 25 minutes.

Hint: Hint: The torta may be reheated, loosely covered with foil, in a 375 degree oven. May also be frozen.

Choctaw-Chickasaw Pashofa

Tishomingo Chickasaw Festival   4 servings

1 pound cracked corn (pearl hominy)
1 pound lean pork back bone
2 quarts water

- Wash and clean corn. Bring water to a boil and add the corn. Cook slowly, stirring often. When corn is about half done, add the fresh pork. Cook until the meat and corn are tender and soft. The mixture should be thick and soupy. Cooking time is about 4 hours. Add no salt while cooking. Each individual salts to his own taste.

Hint: If meaty back bone is not available, use fresh chopped pork. Pork chops are also good to use.

An old-time Indian recipe and Southwest favorite. Try it for supper on a cold, wintry night. But don't forget the Chickasaw Fry Bread.

151

Sausage and Mushroom Quiche

Patty Withrow   12 servings

2 9-inch pastry shells, unbaked
1 pound sausage
1 pound small mushrooms, cut in half
½ cup parsley, minced
4 eggs
½ teaspoon salt
2 cups light cream
1 cup Parmesan cheese, grated

- Preheat oven to 400 degrees. Crumble sausage in large skillet. Add mushrooms and cook, stirring frequently until meat and mushrooms are lightly browned and all liquid has evaporated. Drain. Add parsley.
- Beat eggs with cream and cheese. Blend into mushroom mixture and stir in salt. Pour into pastry shells.
- Bake until crust is browned and filling is set, 25 to 30 minutes. Let stand 10 minutes before cutting. Serve with salad.
- Quiche freezes well before or after cooking and may be reheated.

New Orleans Muffuletta Sandwich

An Oklahoma tail-gate party favorite!

Carol David   4 servings

½ cup stuffed olives, chopped
½ cup dry, oil cured olives, pitted and diced
½ cup mixed pickled vegetables, drained and chopped
¼ cup parsley, minced
½ cup olive oil
3 tablespoons lemon juice
1 garlic clove, minced
1 teaspoon oregano
fresh ground pepper, to taste
1 round, 10-inch loaf Italian bread, split
¼ pound salami, thinly sliced
¼ pound Provolone cheese, sliced
4 slices prosciutto

- Combine olives, vegetables, parsley, oil, lemon juice, garlic, oregano and pepper. Chop in food processor.
- Cover olive mixture. Refrigerate overnight, tossing once or twice.
- To assemble sandwich, remove a little bread from cut sides, forming 2 shells. Brush cut sides of bread with marinade. Layer bottom with salami, half the olive mixture, the Provolone, remaining olive mixture and the prosciutto.
- Cover with bread top. Wrap in foil and weight with heavy object. Place in refrigerator. To serve, cut in wedges.

Moussaka

Eleanor Ferris   4 servings

1 eggplant, sliced
salt
2 tablespoons olive oil
4 medium onions
2 pounds cooked beef or lamb,
minced
4 tomatoes, peeled and sliced
½ cup chicken stock
½ cup tomato purée
2 eggs
1 pint plain yogurt
salt and pepper, to taste

- Preheat oven to 350 degrees.
- Sprinkle eggplant with salt and sauté in skillet with a little olive oil. Spray bottom of a casserole dish with cooking spray. Arrange slices of eggplant in bottom of dish.
- Slice onions and sauté in same skillet until lightly browned. Place layers of onion and minced meat on top of eggplant slices.
- Sauté tomato in skillet and add to casserole. Mix chicken stock and tomato purée and pour over the layered ingredients.
- Bake for 30 minutes. Remove from oven. Beat together the eggs, yogurt, salt and pepper and pour over casserole. Return to oven for 20 minutes or until sauce is set firm and golden brown.

Grilled Rack of Lamb

Sue Hood   8 servings

4 racks of lamb, trimmed and scored
¼ cup chicken bouillon
1 ½ cups honey
¼ cup Worcestershire sauce
½ cup Dijon mustard
1 teaspoon dried marjoram

- Wipe lamb with damp paper towels.
- Mix remaining ingredients; spread over meat and marinate at room temperature 2 to 3 hours.
- Drain the lamb when ready to grill, reserving the marinade. Grill 25 to 35 minutes, basting with the marinade several times. Turn the lamb twice during grilling.

Calories per serving: 255	
Saturated Fat 4 g	Cholesterol 84 mg
Total Fat 12 g (43% of Calories)	Sodium 354 mg

Nettie's Leg of Lamb

Nettie Williams   10 servings

1 7to8 pound leg of lamb
4 garlic cloves, cut in slivers
1 cup of herbs (a blend of dried mint, basil, tarragon, parsley, oregano and chives)
lemon juice to moisten herbs
3 pounds medium white potatoes, pared
2 cups brewed coffee

- Preheat oven to 350 degrees.
- Cut small pockets in the flesh of lamb and fill each with a sliver of garlic. Place the lamb on a rack in a roasting pan. Cover the top of the lamb with the herb and lemon juice mixture.
- Place the potatoes around the lamb. Bake for 25 minutes per pound. After one hour of baking, pour coffee over the lamb.

Hint: Serve with Mint Sauce.

Variation: Make a paste of 3 tablespoons lemon juice, 3 minced garlic buds, 1 tablespoon curry, salt and pepper. Rub over the lamb. For the last 1 ½ hours of roasting, add ⅔ cup of dry vermouth.

Nettie is the founder and conductor of the Metropolitan Chorus of Oklahoma City and the wife of Oklahoma City Philharmonic principal bass player, John Williams.

Lamb Chops Teriyaki

Joanna Todd   4 servings

8 loin or rib lamb chops
½ cup Worcestershire sauce
½ cup Teriyaki sauce
2 garlic cloves, mashed
1 teaspoon fresh or dried tarragon,
minced

- Trim fat from the chops and place in a gallon sealable plastic bag. Whisk rest of ingredients together and pour over the chops in the bag. Seal and let chops marinate for 2 to 3 hours at room temperature.

- While the grill coals are heating, drain the marinade and discard. Over hot coals, grill the chops 4 minutes on each side for medium done and 6 minutes each side for well done. Accompany with fresh Mint Sauce.

MINT SAUCE
¼ cup finely chopped fresh mint leaves
2 teaspoons sugar or two packets NutraSweet
⅓ cup heated malt vinegar
3 tablespoons hot water
salt to taste

- Whisk all ingredients together. Taste and adjust quantities if necessary. Cover and let stand at room temperature for several hours.

155

Spring Lamb Stew

Barbara Tunell   8 servings

4 pounds breast of lamb, 1-inch
cubes
1 teaspoon salt
¼ teaspoon pepper
2 tablespoons vegetable oil
1 garlic clove, crushed
1 onion, minced
2 tablespoon flour
2 ½ cups water
2 large tomatoes, peeled and diced
1 tablespoon salt
2 tablespoon butter
3 to 6 carrots, 1-inch chunks
6 medium turnips, 1-inch chunks
12 white boiling onions
½ teaspoon sugar
12 tiny new potatoes
1 cup frozen green peas, thawed
1 cup frozen green beans, thawed

- Sprinkle lamb with 1 teaspoon salt and the pepper. Heat oil in a large heavy stew pot and sauté lamb until brown. Remove from pot and set aside.

- Add garlic, minced onion and flour to the pot and cook over low heat until flour is lightly browned. Add water, tomatoes, the tablespoon of salt and the sautéed lamb.

- Simmer, covered, 45 minutes or until meat is tender.

- In a large skillet, melt butter and add carrots, turnips, and onions. Sprinkle with sugar and sauté until lightly browned. Add these vegetables and the new potatoes to the stew pot. Simmer, covered, for 30 minutes.

- Add peas and beans and simmer until they are heated through, 5 to 6 minutes.

Shepherd's Pie

JoAnn Arneson   6 servings

**4 large baking potatoes, baked and
cooled slightly
3 tablespoons butter
¼ teaspoon dried tarragon
1 egg yolk, beaten
2 tablespoons bacon fat or oil
1 ½ pounds lean lamb, cut into
small cubes
3 to 6 tablespoons rich lamb or
beef stock
¼ teaspoon Worcestershire sauce
1 tablespoon minced green onion
tops
1 large onion, chopped
6 tablespoons dried tarragon
salt and pepper to taste
butter, optional**

- Preheat oven to 375 degrees.
- Split potatoes in half and scoop pulp into bowl. Add butter, green onion, tarragon, salt and pepper and blend well. Cool to luke-warm, then whip in egg yolk thoroughly. Set aside.
- Butter a deep, 1 ½-quart baking dish. Heat fat or oil in large skillet over medium high heat. Add onion and sauté until softened. Increase heat to high; add lamb and sauté 2 minutes.
- Stir in stock, Worcestershire and tarragon. Remove from heat, taste and adjust seasoning.
- Spread ⅔ of potato mixture over bottom and sides of prepared dish. Add lamb mixture with all juices. Spread remaining potatoes evenly over top, covering completely. Dot with butter, if desired, and bake about 1 ½ hours.
- May be assembled and refrigerated up to 2 days before baking. Potato skins may be frozen, cut into small pieces, deep fried and served as an appetizer.

Pheasant Normandie

Cissy Long   4 servings

¼ **pound bacon slices**
1 **large pheasant, dressed**
4 **tablespoons butter, melted**
1 **pound cooking apples, peeled,**
cored and thickly sliced
¼ **pound fresh mushrooms, sliced**
salt and pepper to taste
½ **cup half and half**
1 ½ **tablespoons Calvados or apple**
brandy

- Preheat oven to 350 degrees. Tie bacon around the pheasant and brown in a large pan with the butter.

- Place pheasant in a casserole dish and layer the apples and mushrooms around it. Season to taste.

- Mix the cream with the Calvados and pour over the pheasant. Cover and bake for one hour, basting the bird occasionally with the juices.

Quail in Wine Sauce

Jody McLane   4 servings

8 quail, dressed
salt and pepper, to taste
3 tablespoons butter
½ cup carrots, diced
½ cup celery, diced
2 tablespoons onion, diced
2 tablespoons green pepper, diced
1 cup fresh mushrooms, sliced
2 medium-sized pieces of orange peel
1 tablespoon flour
1 cup chicken stock
½ cup dry white wine

- Preheat oven to 450 degrees. Sprinkle quail with salt and pepper. Heat butter in a large skillet and brown the quail on all sides. Transfer to a buttered casserole dish.

- In the same skillet, over low heat, add carrots, celery, onion, pepper and mushrooms. Blanch orange peel in hot water and add to the vegetables. Cook 5 minutes. Gradually add the chicken stock, stirring until the sauce thickens. Season with salt and pepper to taste. Simmer 10 minutes.

- Pour wine over the quail and bake 10 to 15 minutes. Reduce the heat to 350 degrees and add the vegetable sauce. Cover and cook 25 minutes, or until the quail is tender. Serve with rice.

Sherried Quail with Mushrooms

Donita Phillips   12 servings

12 quail, dressed
milk to cover the quail
salt, red and black pepper, to taste
flour to dredge quail
vegetable oil
1 medium onion, chopped
6 green onions, chopped
2 tablespoons vegetable oil
8 ounces fresh mushrooms, sliced
3 tablespoons flour
2 ¼ cups chicken bouillon
8 ounces small fresh mushrooms,
whole
2 tablespoons butter
½ cup celery, chopped
2 garlic cloves, crushed
1 cup dry sherry, divided

- Place quail in a large casserole in a single layer. Pour milk over quail to cover. Seal with plastic wrap and place in refrigerator overnight.

- When ready to cook quail, drain well and sprinkle with salt and pepper. Dredge quail with flour.

- Heat ½ inch oil in a large, deep skillet. Brown the quail on all sides. Remove from pan and drain on paper towels. Set aside.

- In a large skillet, sauté onions in 2 tablespoons oil until softened. Add sliced mushrooms and sauté for 3 minutes. Stir in 3 table-spoons flour and cook until flour has lightly browned. Add the bouillon and simmer, stirring fre-quently, for about 30 minutes.

- Meanwhile, in a small skillet sauté whole mushrooms in butter until softened.

- To the large skillet with bouillon mixture, add whole mushrooms, celery, garlic and ½ cup sherry. Cook 15 minutes. Add the quail and remaining ½ cup sherry. Simmer, covered, for 1-2 hours. Best after 24 hours, so it's good to prepare this dish ahead. Serve over wild rice.

Wild Goose

Jane Harlow   6 servings

1 goose, cleaned
1 to 1 ½ strips bacon for each piece
of goose
1 medium onion, coarsely chopped
½ green pepper, chopped
1 to 2 garlic cloves, chopped
½ cup wine, red or white
1 teaspoon Worcestershire sauce
¾ teaspoon sage
¾ cup chicken broth

- Preheat oven to 325 degrees. Cut goose into serving size pieces. Soak in cold water, changing often, for 2 to 4 hours.

- Partially cook bacon in skillet. Remove from pan and save. Add vegetables and sauté until onion is translucent.

- Discard most of fat in pan and deglaze with wine and chicken broth. Add sage and Worcestershire sauce.

- Bring mixture to a boil and simmer with vegetables for about 5 minutes.

- Arrange goose in baking dish and cover with bacon.

- Pour vegetable-wine mixture over goose and bake for 1 ½ hours or until tender.

Warm Duck Salad

Stan Zerbst   4 servings

1 duck, cooked, boned and julienned
1 pound endive lettuce, large shred
2 oranges, peeled and sectioned
½ cup Raspberry Walnut Vinaigrette, well blended
cranberries or grapes and walnuts to garnish

- Line a large platter, which is at room temperature, with the endive.
- Arrange the duck meat in the center of the platter on top of the endive. Ladle Raspberry Walnut Vinaigrette over half of the duck.
- Arrange the orange slices, alternated with cranberries or grapes, around the duck, and garnish the edges of the platter with walnut halves. Serve with additional vinaigrette.

RASPBERRY WALNUT VINAIGRETTE
¼ cup red wine vinegar
¼ cup frozen raspberries
½ cup vegetable oil
1 cup walnut oil
salt and white pepper to taste

- Whisk to blend ingredients thoroughly, then strain to remove the seeds.

Chef Zerbst is the Executive Chef at Oklahoma City's Sportsman's Club, which has extensive hunting and fishing leases throughout Oklahoma.

Oklahoma Brunch Casserole

Rachel McGee   12 servings

1 box (6 ounce) seasoned croutons
2 pounds pork sausage
1 cup sharp Cheddar cheese, grated
1 can (4 ounce) sliced mushrooms, drained
1 can (4 ounce) diced green chiles, drained
2 cups milk
8 eggs
1 teaspoon dry mustard
1 can (10 ounce) cream of mushroom soup

- Preheat oven to 325 degrees. Coat a 9x13-inch glass baking dish with vegetable spray.
- Layer croutons, sausage, cheese, mushrooms and chiles in baking dish in the order listed.
- Beat milk and eggs together until frothy. Stir dry mustard and soup together until well mixed and add to egg mixture. Stir together to blend and pour over layered ingredients.
- Refrigerate several hours or overnight. Bake for 1 hour.

Cheddar Jack Cheese Pie

Pat Hosty   8 servings

1 ¾ cups Monterey Jack cheese, shredded
1 cup mild Cheddar cheese, shredded
1 can (4 ounce) chopped green chiles
1 cup half and half
3 eggs, slightly beaten
¼ teaspoon salt
⅛ teaspoon cumin
½ teaspoon cayenne pepper (optional)
1 10-inch pie crust, baked only 10 minutes

- Preheat oven to 325 degrees.
- Sprinkle Monterey Jack cheese and half of Cheddar cheese in pie shell. Arrange chiles over cheese.
- Beat half and half together with eggs, cumin and cayenne. Pour over cheeses. Sprinkle remaining Cheddar over pie filling and bake for 40 minutes.

Asparagus Quiche

Debbie Ritter   6 servings

1 8 to 9-inch unbaked pie shell
1 pound fresh asparagus
8 ounces fresh mushrooms, sliced
¼ cup grated Parmesan cheese
1 cup shredded Swiss cheese
4 eggs, whisked
1 small can Milnot (⅔ cup)
½ teaspoon salt
½ teaspoon white pepper
¼ teaspoon nutmeg
2 tablespoons Worcestershire sauce

- Preheat oven to 375 degrees. Prick air holes in bottom and sides of pastry shell and bake 10 minutes. Remove from oven and cool.

- In pie shell, layer asparagus, mushrooms, Parmesan and Swiss cheeses.

- Mix eggs and Milnot with wire whisk. Add remaining ingredients and pour over layers in pie shell.

- Place pie shell on cookie sheet and bake in 325 degree oven for 45 minutes, or until set in center and light brown around outer edges.

Homemade Egg Substitute

Colleen Blaylock Green   ¾ cup

6 egg whites
¼ cup instant nonfat dry milk
2 tablespoons water
1 ½ teaspoons vegetable oil
¼ teaspoon ground turmeric

- Combine all ingredients in container of blender or food processor. Process 30 seconds only.

- Refrigerate up to 1 week or freeze in an airtight container up to 1 month.

Hint: There are 90 calories for each ¼ cup. Using low cholesterol oil, this has 2.4 grams fat.

Nancy's Deviled Egg Brunch

Nancy Whitter   6 servings

6 eggs, hard boiled
¼ cup celery, chopped
1 tablespoon mayonnaise
1 teaspoon prepared mustard
6 slices cooked ham
1 can cream of mushroom soup
⅓ cup milk
½ cup Cheddar cheese, grated
¼ cup potato chips, crushed
sliced stuffed olives for garnish

- Preheat oven to 350 degrees.
- Slice eggs and remove yolks.
- Combine yolks, celery, mayonnaise and mustard. Refill whites. Put halves together and wrap each egg with ham slice. Arrange with folded side down.
- Combine soup and milk. Pour over ham rolls. Sprinkle with cheese and potato chips and top with olives.
- Bake for 30 minutes. Serve immediately.

Wine Eggs Mornay

Nancy Apgar   6 servings

WINE MORNAY SAUCE
3 tablespoons butter
3 tablespoons flour
¾ teaspoon salt
¼ teaspoon nutmeg
dash pepper
1 cup light cream
¼ cup dry white wine
⅓ cup Swiss cheese, shredded

- Melt butter. Blend in flour, salt, nutmeg and pepper. Add cream, all at once. Cook quickly, stirring constantly, till mixture thickens and bubbles.
- Add white wine and cheese and stir to melt.
  Yield: 1 ⅓ cups

6 thin slices cooked ham (or Canadian bacon)
3 English muffins, split in half, toasted and buttered
6 eggs, poached
1 tablespoon green pepper, finely chopped
1 tablespoon snipped chives

- Lightly brown ham in a little butter. Place one slice on each muffin half. Place poached egg atop each ham slice. Season.
- Pour Wine Mornay Sauce over eggs. Sprinkle with pepper and chives.

Low Fat Chile Rellenos Casserole

Dolores Boyle   8 servings

**2 cans (4 ounce) chopped green
chiles
1 package (8 ounce) low fat
Cheddar cheese, shredded
1 carton (8 ounce) egg substitute
2 cups skim milk
1 cup packaged biscuit mix
1 cup low fat cottage cheese
salsa (optional)**

Calories per serving: 325
Saturated Fat 4 g
Cholesterol 22 mg
Total Fat 11 g (32% of Calories)
Sodium 783 mg

- Preheat oven to 350 degrees. Coat a 9x13-inch baking dish with cooking spray.

- Spread chiles on bottom of dish, then layer with the cheese. Set aside.

- In medium bowl, whisk eggs, milk and biscuit mix until smooth. Stir in cottage cheese. Spoon egg mixture over chiles and cheese.

- Bake uncovered for 45 minutes, or until puffed and knife inserted near center comes out clean. Let stand 10 minutes. Serve with salsa, if desired.

A modern day adaptation of a dish from Dolores' Restaurant which brings back fond memories of old Route 66 in Oklahoma City.

Meatless Spinach Lasagna

Pat Higgins   10 servings

2 packages (10 ounce) frozen
spinach
¼ cup olive oil
3 garlic cloves, minced
1 teaspoon basil
1 teaspoon oregano
salt and pepper to taste
1 package (8 ounce) lasagna noodles
1 carton (12 ounce) ricotta cheese
1 quart spaghetti sauce without
meat
1 pound whole milk mozzarella
cheese, shredded
¾ cup Parmesan cheese, grated

- Preheat oven to 350 degrees. Grease a 3-quart baking dish.

- Thaw spinach and squeeze to remove moisture. Add olive oil, garlic, basil, oregano, salt and pepper. Mix to blend.

- Cook lasagna according to directions, drain and moisten with olive oil.

- In baking dish, layer half the lasagna noodles, half the spinach mixture, half the ricotta, half the spaghetti sauce and half the mozzarella cheese. Repeat layers and top with Parmesan cheese.

- Bake 30 minutes. Let stand 10 minutes before serving.

Variations: Sautéed vegetables such as eggplant, zucchini and onion may be used instead of the spinach, in any desired combination.

Twenty Four Hour Omelet

Misha Dichter   12 servings

1 long loaf day old French bread,
broken in small pieces
6 tablespoons unsalted butter,
melted
¾ pound Swiss cheese, shredded
½ pound Monterey Jack, shredded
9 slices Genoa salami, chopped
16 eggs
3 ¼ cups milk
½ cup white wine
4 scallions, minced
1 tablespoon German mustard
¼ tablespoon ground pepper
½ tablespoon cayenne pepper
1 ½ cup sour cream
1 cup Parmesan cheese, freshly
grated

- Butter two shallow 9x13-inch baking dishes. Spread bread over bottom and drizzle with butter. Sprinkle with cheeses and meats.
- Beat together eggs, milk, wine, scallions, mustard and peppers. Pour over cheese. Cover with foil. Refrigerate overnight.
- Remove from refrigerator 30 minutes before baking. Preheat oven to 325 degrees and bake 1 hour. Uncover and spread with sour cream and sprinkle with Parmesan.
- Return to oven until lightly brown, about 10 minutes.

Variations: Smoked salmon or vegetables may be used in place of Genoa salami.

M isha Dichter is an internationally renowned concert pianist, always welcomed back to Oklahoma with great applause.

Southwestern Omelet

Jill Mizel   10 servings

1 ¼ pound package frozen hash browns
1 ½ pound sausage or ham
1 can (4 ounce) chopped green chiles
1 jar (4 ounce) pimentos
½ pound Monterey Jack cheese, shredded
12 eggs
½ cup milk
1 cup mushrooms, sautéed

- Preheat oven to 350 degrees.

- Bake hash browns according to package directions or sauté in a small amount of butter. Distribute evenly in a 9x13-inch baking dish.

- If using sausage, cook and crumble. Layer meat (sausage or ham) over potatoes.

- Mix chiles, pimentos and mushrooms and distribute evenly over meat. Sprinkle cheese over layers.

- Whisk eggs and milk together and pour over layered ingredients.

- Bake for 45 to 60 minutes, until eggs are of desired texture.

Breakfast Soufflé

Kathryn Steely   8 servings

8 slices bacon, diced
4 tablespoons butter
2 packages (3 ounce) chipped beef,
coarsely shredded
½ pound fresh mushrooms, sliced
and lightly sautéed in butter
½ cup flour
¼ teaspoon pepper
1 quart milk
12 eggs, lightly beaten
2 cups Monterey Jack cheese,
grated
¼ teaspoon salt
¾ cup milk or half and half
4 tablespoons butter, melted

- Preheat oven to 350 degrees. Butter a 9-inch soufflé dish.

- Cook bacon and discard fat from skillet. Remove skillet from heat and add butter, chipped beef, and ¾ of the mushrooms.

- Mix well and sprinkle with flour and pepper. Gradually add milk, then the cheese, cooking and stirring until mixture is thickened and smooth. Cover and set aside.

- Combine eggs, salt, and ¾ cup milk. Cook in butter until softly scrambled; do not overcook or eggs will be dry.

- In the prepared dish, layer eggs and sauce twice, ending with sauce. Garnish with remaining mushrooms and bake for 15 to 20 minutes.

DESSERTS

THE GILCREASE MUSEUM

The Thomas Gilcrease Institute of American History and Art in Tulsa houses one of the nation's foremost collections of Western art. Artifacts, art, rare books and documents illustrate the development of Western Americana from pre-Columbian times through the last century. Containing works by Remington, Russell, Audubon, Catlin, Moran and many others, the Gilcrease is one of the most important museums of its kind in the world.

Fresh Apple Cake

Wonderful for Christmas brunch.

Mary Braum   12 to 16 servings

½ cup shortening
2 cups sugar
2 eggs, beaten
2 cups flour
½ teaspoon salt
1 teaspoon soda
1 teaspoon cinnamon
1 teaspoon nutmeg
4 cups apples, peeled and finely chopped
1 cup dates, chopped
2 cups nuts, chopped

- Preheat oven to 300 degrees. Grease and flour 9x13-inch pan.

- Cream sugar and shortening. Add eggs, mixing well.

- Sift together flour, salt, soda, cinnamon and nutmeg. Add to creamed ingredients. Stir in apples, nuts and dates.

- Pour into prepared pan and bake 50 minutes or until brown.

- Serve warm with whipped cream.

In Tuttle, Oklahoma, the Braum Family has one of the largest, state of the art dairy facilities in the world..a featured stop when touring the state.

Dancer's Delight

Betty Burnham   16 to 20 servings

4 eggs, separated
2 cups sugar
¾ cup butter
2 cups cake flour, sifted
½ cup whipping cream
1 teaspoon butter flavoring
1 tablespoon bourbon
1 teaspoon vanilla extract
1 tablespoon vegetable oil

Betty danced in the Ballet Russe with Oklahoma's prima ballerina, Yvonne Choteau. Along the way, she studied cooking in Paris at the Cordon Bleu.

- Preheat oven to 325 degrees. Grease and flour a bundt cake pan.
- Beat egg whites until stiff, then chill. In large mixing bowl, cream butter and sugar. Using mixer on low, add egg yolks alternately with cream, flour, oil and flavorings. After blending, turn mixer to high for 3 to 5 minutes.
- Gently fold in egg whites. Do not overbeat. Pour batter into pan and smooth gently until top is level.
- Bake in center of oven 1 hour and 10 minutes. Cool 10 minutes and invert onto plate.

Pear Cake

Kathleen Howe Bressie   12 servings

3 large very ripe pears
2 cups sugar
3 eggs, well beaten
1 ½ cups vegetable oil
3 cups flour
1 teaspoon baking soda
1 teaspoon salt
2 teaspoons cinnamon
1 teaspoon vanilla extract
confectioner's sugar

- Preheat oven to 350 degrees. Grease a 10-inch bundt cake pan.
- Peel and thinly slice the pears, or mash in a food processor.
- Combine sugar, eggs and oil in a large mixing bowl. Mix well.
- In a small bowl, mix dry ingredients and stir into the egg mixture. Add vanilla and fold in pears.
- Spoon batter into pan and bake for 1 hour and 10 minutes. Cake should be brown and pull away from sides.
- Let cake cool 10 to 15 minutes on a rack. Invert onto cake plate and dust with confectioner's sugar.

Lemon Fruit Cake

Ethel Findlay   12 servings

2 cups pecans, halves or chopped
½ box white raisins
4 cups flour, divided
2 cups butter
2 ½ cups sugar
6 eggs
1 heaping teaspoon baking powder
1 bottle (2 ounce) lemon extract

- Preheat oven to 250 degrees. Grease and flour a 10-inch tube pan.
- Place nuts and raisins in a small mixing bowl, then sprinkle ½ cup of the flour over them, stirring to coat well. This will insure that the nuts and raisins do not sink to the bottom of pan during baking. Set aside.
- Using an electric mixer, cream the butter and sugar until light and mixture is no longer grainy. Add eggs one at a time, mixing well.
- Stir baking powder into remaining 3 ½ cups flour and blend into batter alternately with lemon extract.
- Add the floured nuts and raisins to the batter, mixing gently by hand.
- Pour batter into prepared tube pan and bake for 3 hours.

EmmyLou's Lemon Poppy Seed Pound Cake

EmmyLou Harris   10 to 12 servings

3 cups flour
2 cups sugar
¼ cup poppy seeds
1 cup butter, softened
1 cup buttermilk
4 eggs
½ teaspoon baking soda
½ teaspoon baking powder
½ teaspoon salt
4 teaspoons freshly grated lemon rind
½ teaspoon vanilla extract

- Preheat oven to 325 degrees. Grease and flour a 12 cup bundt pan or 10-inch tube pan.
- In large bowl, combine all cake ingredients.
- Beat at low speed, scraping bowl often, until all ingredients are moistened. Then beat at high speed, scraping bowl often, until smooth (1 to 2 minutes).
- Pour into prepared pan and bake 55 to 65 minutes or until toothpick inserted in center comes out clean.
- Cool 10 minutes and remove from pan. Cool completely.

GLAZE
1 cup powdered sugar
1 to 2 tablespoons lemon juice, freshly squeezed

- In small bowl, stir together powdered sugar and lemon juice until smooth. Drizzle over cake.

EmmyLou Harris is not only a crowd dazzler, her cake will be applauded at your next dinner party.

Coffee Angel Food Cake

An adaptation of a Zodiac Room favorite!

Jacquelyn Stengel   12 to 16 servings

1 angel food cake mix
1 tablespoon instant coffee
2 tablespoons water

- Move oven rack to lowest position and preheat oven to 375 degrees.

- Beat angel food cake mix with water as directed on the package. When mixture begins to form soft peaks, stir in coffee dissolved in 2 tablespoons water. Continue beating until stiff peaks form,

- Pour batter into an ungreased angel food cake pan. With a narrow spatula, cut through batter to remove large air bubbles.

- Bake 30 to 40 minutes or until golden brown. Don't overbake.

- Invert on bottle to cool. Very carefully loosen sides with a thin knife before removing.

QUICK COFFEE ICING
1 can (15 ounce) creamy vanilla
frosting
2 teaspoons instant coffee
1 tablespoon milk or cream
⅓ cup sliced almonds, toasted

- Mix frosting with coffee dissolved in milk. Spread over cake. Pat toasted almonds on sides. This cake freezes beautifully and may be sliced while frozen.

177

Philbrook's Italian Cream Cake

Jody Walls   12 servings

1 cup buttermilk
1 teaspoon soda
½ cup butter
½ cup shortening
2 cups sugar
5 eggs, separated
2 cups flour, sifted
1 teaspoon vanilla extract
3 ½ ounces coconut
1 cup pecans, chopped

- Preheat oven to 350 degrees. Grease and flour three 9-inch cake pans.
- Combine buttermilk and soda and set aside.
- Cream butter, shortening and sugar. Add egg yolks, one at a time, beating after each addition.
- Alternately, add buttermilk and flour, small amounts at a time. Add vanilla extract.
- Beat egg whites to stiff peaks; fold into batter and flour mixture. Stir in coconut and pecans.
- Bake for 25 minutes. Cool on racks.

ICING

1 package (8 ounce) cream cheese, softened
8 cups confectioner's sugar, sifted
1 ½ cups pecans, chopped
1 cup butter, softened
3 teaspoons vanilla extract

- In mixer, cream together cream cheese and butter.
- Add sugar slowly to spreading consistency. Add pecans and vanilla. Frost cake.

Tulsa's beautiful Philbrook Museum reopened its restaurant with a new name and an exciting new creative menu. This delicate cream cake, a creation of their Executive Chef, Jody Walls, appears often at their Sunday Brunch.

French Meringue Cake

Libby Britton   8 servings

6 egg whites, room temperature
2 cups sugar
¾ cup pecans, ground
1 ½ teaspoons white wine vinegar
½ teaspoon vanilla extract

FILLING AND ICING
3 ounces semisweet chocolate
1 ½ cups heavy cream, divided
semisweet chocolate, grated or
cocoa for garnish

- Preheat oven to 350 degrees.

- Cut two rounds of parchment paper to fit the bottoms of two 8-inch round cake pans. Grease and flour the paper generously, then grease and flour the cake pans. Place a paper round in each pan.

- In a large bowl beat egg whites until stiff. Add sugar and nuts, all at once, folding gently with a spatula. Then fold in vinegar and vanilla.

- Spoon batter equally into the two prepared cake pans.

- Bake 40 to 45 minutes or until golden brown and crusty to touch. Watch to avoid burning.

- Remove from oven and immediately run a knife around the edges. Turn upside down on cake racks to cool. Remove pans and carefully peel off paper. You will lose some of the meringue as you peel. Allow to cool.

- Melt the chocolate with ¼ cup cream in the top of a double boiler over hot, not boiling, water. Set aside to cool slightly.

- Whip the remaining cream in a separate bowl until stiff. Carefully fold half the cream into the chocolate mixture.

- Place one meringue round on serving platter and cover with this mixture. Top with second meringue and cover the top with the rest of the whipped cream.

- With a spatula, dip into remaining chocolate and make swirls on the cream to give it a marbled effect. Sprinkle with grated chocolate or cocoa to garnish.

- Chill well, at least four hours, before serving. The chocolate hardens in the cream in this cake, giving it a crunchy texture.

179

Black Satin Fudge Cake

Edward Russell   10 to 12 servings

1 cup butter
6 ounces unsweetened chocolate
6 ounces semisweet chocolate
5 eggs, room temperature
1 cup sugar, divided
⅓ cup light corn syrup

**VALENTINO'S WHITE
CHOCOLATE CUSTARD SAUCE**
7 egg yolks, room temperature
2 tablespoons sugar
1 teaspoon cornstarch
2 ½ cups milk
**6 ounces white chocolate, prefer-
ably Tobler Narcisse, finely
chopped**
**2 tablespoons light Crème de
Cacao**

- Preheat oven to 350 degrees.
- Butter a 9 or 9 ½-inch spring form pan, cutting a circle of waxed paper to fit the bottom. Butter the paper. Wrap outside of pan in foil to keep the batter from seeping out as it bakes.
- In a medium saucepan over low heat, melt butter with all the chocolate, stirring until smooth.
- Set aside to cool slightly.
- In a large mixing bowl with an electric mixer, beat eggs with ½ cup sugar on high speed until light and fluffy, about 5 minutes.
- Meanwhile, in a small saucepan, stir together corn syrup and remaining ½ cup sugar. Bring to a boil over moderate heat and transfer to a heatproof glass measuring cup. Slowly pour hot sugar syrup in a thin, steady stream into the eggs, beating with the mixer on medium speed. On low speed, mix in chocolate until incorporated. Pour into prepared pan.
- Place the springform in a shallow roasting pan in which you have 1 inch of hot water. Bake for 45 minutes or until a toothpick inserted in the center comes out clean. Do not overbake as the cake will firm up as it cools. Remove from water and cool on rack for 30 minutes. Invert onto a plate and serve with Valentino's White Chocolate Custard Sauce.
- In a large bowl with an electric mixer on medium speed, beat egg yolks and sugar until very thick and light colored, about 3 minutes. Mix in cornstarch.
- Meanwhile, in a heavy deep saucepan, heat milk until small bubbles appear around the sides. Remove from heat, stir in chocolate and liqueur until smooth. Gradually stir about 1 ½ cups of the milk chocolate mixture into the yolks to warm them, then pour the yolk mixture into the chocolate. Cook over medium low heat, stirring constantly with a wooden spoon, until the custard thickens slightly. It is done when you can run your finger down the back of the spoon and a path remains down the custard for several seconds. Do not let it boil.
- To serve, place the white chocolate sauce on the bottom of a dessert plate and place a wedge of the chocolate cake on top. Garnish with fresh berries and a sprig of mint.

Mr. Russell's outstanding catering facility, Valentino's, serves this cake to rave audiences.

Prohibition Whiskey Cake

The more you eat, the more you want!

Marge Duncan   12 servings

½ cup butter, softened
1 cup sugar
3 eggs, beaten
1 cup flour
½ teaspoon baking powder
¼ teaspoon salt
½ teaspoon nutmeg
¼ cup milk
¼ cup molasses
¼ teaspoon baking soda
1 pound seedless raisins
2 cups pecans, chopped
¼ cup bourbon whiskey

- Preheat oven to 300 degrees. Grease and flour a loaf pan or bundt pan.
- Cream the butter and sugar and add the beaten eggs.
- Mix together flour, baking powder, salt and nutmeg, add to the creamed mixture. Add the milk, mixing well.
- Combine the baking soda and molasses and add to the batter. Stir in the raisins, nuts and whiskey.
- Pour into the prepared pan and bake for two hours.

Hint: The cake will keep well, wrapped in foil and refrigerated. Perk it up by jabbing with an ice pick and injecting a little more bourbon.

Chocolate on Chocolate Cheesecake

Ann Taylor   12 servings

1 package (9 ounce) chocolate
wafers
⅓ cup butter, melted
2 tablespoons sugar
¼ teaspoon nutmeg

- Chop wafers fine in food processor. Add melted butter, sugar and nutmeg and blend well.

- Pat into bottom of 9-inch springform pan. Refrigerate.

- Preheat oven to 350 degrees.

FILLING
3 packages (8 ounce) cream cheese,
softened
2 packages (6 ounce) semisweet
chocolate chips, melted
1 cup sour cream
1 cup sugar
⅛ teaspoon salt
1 tablespoon vanilla extract
3 eggs, beaten

- In the same food processing bowl, blend cream cheese, chocolate, sour cream, sugar, salt and vanilla extract. When well blended, add eggs one at a time. Pour mixture on top of cold crumb mix.

- Bake 1 hour or until firm. Cool in pan. Refrigerate at least 1 hour before slicing to serve. Dollops of whipped cream and sliced almonds are a nice touch. This is a favorite for large family dinners because it can be made ahead. Delicious!

Golden Lemon Glazed Cheesecake

Another award winning recipe

Clella Lookabaugh   16 servings

CRUST
2 ½ cups graham cracker crumbs
¼ cup sugar
10 tablespoons butter, melted

FILLING
3 packages (8 ounce) cream cheese, softened
3 eggs
1 ¼ cups sugar
3 tablespoons fresh lemon juice
1 teaspoon vanilla extract
1 tablespoon grated lemon peel

GLAZE
1 lemon, sliced paper thin
3 cups water, divided
1 cup sugar
2 tablespoons, plus 2 teaspoons cornstarch
⅓ cup fresh lemon juice

- Preheat oven to 350 degrees.
- Combine all crust ingredients and press into the bottom and 2 inches up the sides of a 9-inch spring-form pan. Bake 5 minutes. Cool.
- In a mixing bowl, beat cream cheese at medium high until smooth. Add eggs, one at a time, beating well after each addition. Gradually add sugar, then lemon juice and vanilla. Mix well. Fold in lemon peel. Pour into crust. Bake 40 minutes. Cool to room temperature, then refrigerate until thoroughly chilled, at least 4 hours.
- Remove any seeds from the lemon slices. Reserve 1 slice for garnish. Coarsely chop remaining slices. Place in a saucepan with 2 cups water. Bring to a boil and simmer, uncovered, for 15 minutes. Drain and discard liquid.
- In a saucepan, combine sugar and cornstarch. Stir in remaining water, lemon juice and lemon pulp. Bring to a boil, stirring constantly and boil 3 minutes. Chill until cool, stirring occasionally. Pour over the cheesecake and garnish with reserved lemon slice. Chill until ready to serve.

Watonga has the only cheese factory in the state and nurtures "Made in Oklahoma" cheese cuisine artists. The Watonga Cheese Festival, an annual event, is a major food festival in Oklahoma.

Pumpkin Cheesecake

Libby Britton   12 to 16 servings

1 ½ cups graham cracker crumbs
2 tablespoons sugar
⅓ cup almonds, toasted and
ground (measure after grinding)
½ teaspoon ginger
½ teaspoon cinnamon
6 tablespoons butter

- Preheat oven to 375 degrees.
- Combine ingredients and press into a 10-inch springform pan.
- Bake 8 minutes. Remove from oven and cool.
- Reduce oven temperature to 325 degrees.

FILLING
4 packages (8 ounce) cream cheese
1 ¼ cups sugar
3 tablespoons maple syrup
3 tablespoons cognac
1 teaspoon ginger
1 teaspoon cinnamon
½ teaspoon nutmeg
4 eggs
¼ cup heavy cream
1 cup canned pumpkin

- All ingredients should be room temperature. Beat softened cream cheese with mixer until smooth. Gradually add sugar. Add maple syrup, cognac, ginger, cinnamon and nutmeg. Beat well. Add eggs, one at a time, beating well after each addition. Add cream and pumpkin and blend well. Pour into prepared crust.
- Bake 45 minutes. Turn oven off. Do not open oven. Leave cake in oven for 1 hour, then remove.
- Preheat oven to 425 degrees.

TOPPING
2 cups sour cream
¼ cup sugar
1 tablespoon maple syrup
1 tablespoon cognac

- Combine ingredients, cover and keep at room temperature while cheesecake is in the oven. Spread topping over cake.
- Bake 10 minutes. Remove from oven and cool at room temperature for 1 hour.
- Remove side of springform pan carefully. Wash and replace around the cake before chilling. Chill at least 3 hours before serving. Garnish with white chocolate leaves.

Gingerbread

Marilyn Ehlers   12 servings

½ cup sugar
½ cup shortening
1 egg
1 cup molasses
1 teaspoon cinnamon
1 teaspoon ginger
½ teaspoon cloves
½ teaspoon salt
2 ½ cups cake flour
1 ½ teaspoon soda
1 cup boiling water

- Preheat oven to 350 degrees. Coat 9x13-inch pan with cooking spray.
- Combine sugar, shortening, egg, molasses, and spices. Beat well with electric mixer until fluffy.
- Stir in flour and soda. Add boiling water. Do not overbeat.
- Bake in prepared pan until firm to touch.

Ranch House Cookies

Libby Britton   8 dozen

1 cup butter, softened
1 cup sugar
1 cup firmly packed brown sugar
1 egg
1 cup vegetable oil
1 teaspoon vanilla extract
3 ½ cups flour, sifted
1 teaspoon baking soda
1 teaspoon salt
½ cup shredded coconut
1 cup quick rolled oats
1 cup pecans, chopped
1 cup plain cornflakes, crushed
1 cup chocolate chips, optional

- Preheat oven to 325 degrees.
- In a mixer, cream the butter and sugars until fluffy. Add the egg, vanilla and oil, mixing well.
- In a separate bowl, combine the flour, baking soda and salt. Add gradually to the butter mixture, mixing well. Add the oats, corn flakes, coconut and nuts, stirring to mix.
- Form the dough into 1-inch balls. Place on an ungreased cookie sheet. Flatten with a fork dipped in water. Bake 10 to 11 minutes, or until golden. Cool on cookie sheets for a few minutes before removing. You may add 1 cup chocolate chips. These cookies freeze well.

APPLAUSE

Lace Cookie Cups
For that special occasion!

Mattie Lee Cory   10 to 12

⅓ **cup maple syrup**
¼ **cup butter**
½ **cup flour**
3 tablespoons sugar
½ **teaspoon vanilla extract**
⅓ **cup pecans, finely chopped**

- Preheat oven to 325 degrees.
- In a saucepan, bring the syrup to a boil. Remove from heat and stir in butter. Add remaining ingredients.
- Drop one tablespoon of the mixture onto an ungreased cookie sheet. Repeat to make three more cookies, 2 inches apart. Bake 15 minutes or until golden. Remove cookie sheet from oven and let cookies cool for one minute only.
- With a large spatula, quickly loosen and turn the cookies over. Mold over tin muffin cups.
- If the cookies get too hard to mold, reheat in the oven a minute to soften. Cool on the mold. Remove and store in a tightly covered container.
- To serve, fill the cups with a scoop of your favorite ice cream or sherbet. Drizzle with chocolate sauce if desired.

Hint: The sky is the limit on garnishes for this pretty dessert; chopped nuts, whipped cream, toffee bits or, for special occasions, liqueurs.

186

Dutch Spritz Cookies

Sidney Weiss   6 dozen

1 cup butter
¾ cup sugar
1 egg, beaten
1 teaspoon vanilla extract
2 ½ cups cake flour
¼ teaspoon salt
½ teaspoon baking powder

- Preheat oven to 425 degrees.
- Cream sugar and butter. Add egg and flavoring, beating until smooth. Sift flour, salt and baking powder and mix in well.
- Roll dough in small balls, place on ungreased cookie sheet. Press each cookie with fork dipped in flour. Bake for 10 minutes or until cookie is delicately browned.

FROSTING
2 cups confectioner's sugar
water
nuts or chocolate to decorate

- Mix powdered sugar with just enough water to moisten.
- While cookies are still hot, dip in frosting, then in nuts or chocolate.

My mother gave this recipe to my bride and it's still a favorite - especially when I return from a concert tour.

Shortbread Cookies
Deliciously different!

Pat Taliaferro   4 to 5 dozen

1 pound sweet cream butter
1 cup white sugar
4 cups flour
extra sugar

- Cream butter and sugar very thoroughly and gradually work in the flour. Form into 2 or 3 rolls, about 1 ½ to 2 inches in diameter, and wrap in wax paper. Refrigerate at least 4 hours or freeze.
- When ready to bake, preheat oven to 300 degrees.
- Cut in thin slices and place on ungreased cookie sheet. Score each cookie carefully with a sharp fork and sprinkle a little sugar on top.
- Bake 25 to 30 minutes. Do not brown as this destroys the delicate butter flavor. Remove quickly to cool on racks.

Hint: Handle carefully since these cookies are very fragile. Store in tight tins.

This recipe is generations old and was given to my mother by a lady from Scotland who was employed at the British Embassy in Washington, D.C. in the 1940's. She insisted it should always be mixed with a wooden spoon.

Almond Crunch Cookies

Nadine Holloway   3 to 4 dozen

1 cup sugar
1 cup confectioner's sugar, sifted
1 cup butter, softened
1 cup vegetable oil
2 eggs
2 ½ teaspoons almond extract
3 ½ cups flour
1 cup whole wheat flour
1 teaspoon baking soda
1 teaspoon salt
1 teaspoon cream of tartar
2 cups almonds, chopped
1 package (6 ounce) almond brickle chips
Sugar

- Combine 1 cup sugar, powdered sugar, butter and oil in a large mixing bowl. Beat at medium speed until blended. Add eggs and almond extract, beating well.

- Combine flours, soda, salt and cream of tartar. Gradually add to creamed mixture, beating just until blended after each addition. Stir in almonds and brickle chips. Chill dough 3 to 4 hours.

- When ready to bake, preheat oven to 350 degrees.

- Shape dough into 1 ½-inch balls and place at least 3 inches apart on ungreased cookie sheets. Flatten cookies with a fork dipped in sugar, making a criss cross pattern.

- Bake 14 to 15 minutes or until lightly browned. Transfer to wire racks to cool.

Jan's Sugar Cookies

Jan Woodson   5 to 6 dozen small cookies

1 cup butter, softened
1 cup confectioner's sugar
1 cup vegetable oil
1 cup sugar
2 eggs, beaten
4 cups flour
1 teaspoon cream of tartar
1 teaspoon vanilla extract
1 teaspoon soda
1 teaspoon salt

- Beat together butter, oil and sugars. Add rest of ingredients, blending well. Refrigerate overnight.

- When ready to bake, preheat oven to 350 degrees.

- Roll dough in walnut size balls and place 1 inch apart on cookie sheet. Bake 8 minutes.

189

Easy, Easy, Sugar Cookies

Priscilla Braun   4 ½ dozen small cookies

1 cup butter
1 cup sugar
½ teaspoon baking soda
1 ½ cups flour
½ teaspoon vinegar

- Preheat oven to 300 degrees.
- All ingredients should be at room temperature. Mix butter, sugar and soda until creamy.
- Add flour and vinegar and mix well. The dough will be soft.
- Line cookie sheet with foil and grease the foil. Drop dough by teaspoonfuls onto the sheet. Press dough onto sheet lightly with fingers.
- Bake for 20 to 25 minutes. Do not brown.

Chocolate Drop Cookies

Ellie Scherlag   7 dozen

½ cup butter
1 ⅔ cups sugar
2 teaspoons vanilla extract
2 eggs, beaten
6 tablespoons cocoa
2 cups flour
2 teaspoons baking powder
½ teaspoon salt
⅓ cup milk
1 cup nuts, chopped, optional

- Cream butter, sugar, vanilla and well beaten eggs.
- Sift all dry ingredients and add to the butter mixture alternately with the milk. Stir in the nuts and chill one hour.
- When ready to bake, preheat oven to 350 degrees.
- Drop by teaspoonfuls onto ungreased cookie sheets and bake 10 to 12 minutes.

Ahoy Chocolate Chip Cookies

Tom Kemper   48 cookies

2 cups butter
2 cups sugar
2 cups brown sugar
4 eggs
1 teaspoon vanilla extract
4 cups flour
5 cups regular oatmeal
1 teaspoon salt
2 teaspoons baking power
2 teaspoons soda
1 package (24 oz) chocolate chips
1 Hershey bar (6 oz), grated
3 cups nuts, chopped

- Preheat oven to 375 degrees.
- Cream together butter and sugars. Add eggs and vanilla, beating well.
- Mix in separately the flour, oatmeal, salt, baking powder and soda. Add chocolate chips, grated Hershey bar and nuts.
- Place golf ball-size scoop of cookie dough on ungreased cookie sheet 2 inches apart. You may flatten with a fork.
- Bake for six minutes, no longer. You will think they are not done after six minutes, but they are! Do not overbake. Cool on the cookie sheet.

Chocolate Russian Drops

Esther Bernstein   4 to 5 dozen

1 ½ cups sugar
2 eggs
2 squares unsweetened chocolate, melted
2 ¾ cups sifted flour
½ teaspoon baking soda
½ teaspoon baking powder
½ teaspoon salt
½ cup butter
½ cup pecans or walnuts, finely chopped
1 cup sour cream

CHOCOLATE MOCHA ICING
¼ cup butter
¼ cup strong coffee
2 cups confectioner's sugar
¼ cup cocoa
½ teaspoon salt
1 teaspoon vanilla extract

- Sift flour, baking soda, baking powder and salt and set aside.
- Cream butter. Gradually beat in sugar and eggs. Add melted chocolate. Stir in sour cream.
- Gradually add dry ingredients, then nuts.
- Chill at least one hour.
- When ready to bake, preheat oven to 425 degrees.
- Drop by rounded teaspoonfuls on lightly greased baking sheet. Bake about 8 to 10 minutes
- Have butter and coffee at room temperature. Sift together sugar, cocoa and salt. Combine all ingredients and beat until smooth and fluffy.

191

Christmas Cookies
A special family tradition!

Dee Downard   6 dozen

1 pound butter
2 ½ cups sugar
2 eggs, beaten
1 tablespoon baking soda
¼ cup water
5 cups flour
¼ teaspoon salt
4 slices candied pineapple,
chopped
3 ounces candied cherries, halved
1 cup white raisins
2 cups pecans, chopped

- Cream butter and sugar together in mixer. Add well beaten eggs.
- Dissolve baking soda in the water and add to the batter, then add the flour and salt. Blend well. Fold in fruit and nuts.
- Divide the dough into five parts and roll each into approximately 2 ½-inch high rolls. Wrap in plastic wrap and refrigerate at least one hour.
- When ready to bake, preheat oven to 400 degrees.
- Slice into ¼-inch slices and place on greased cookie sheets. Bake 8 to 10 minutes or until light brown.

Walnut Squares

Marion DeVore   30 squares

1 cup bread crumbs, finely ground
¾ cup brown sugar, packed
4 egg whites
½ teaspoon cream of tartar
1 teaspoon vanilla extract
½ cup of walnuts, chopped

- Preheat oven to 350 degrees.
- Mix together bread crumbs and sugar.
- In a separate bowl, beat egg whites with cream of tartar until stiff. Gently fold the vanilla, crumb mixture and walnuts (in order listed) into the egg whites. Bake in an ungreased 8x8-inch pan for 20 minutes, then reduce heat to 300 degrees and bake an additional 10 minutes. Cut into ½-inch squares.

192

New Year's Cookies

Mennonite Community of Corn   4 to 5 dozen

⅓ cup warm water
2 packages dry yeast
1 tablespoon sugar
4 eggs, beaten
½ cup sugar
½ cup butter
3 cups milk, scalded
½ cup cream or top milk
2 cups raisins
8 to 9 cups flour

- Soften yeast in warm water with one tablespoon sugar. Set aside.

- Beat eggs. Add sugar, butter, cream and milk which has been cooled to warm temperature. Mix ½ cup of the flour with the raisins and set aside.

- Add yeast and enough of the remaining flour to the mixture to make a soft spongy dough.

- Add raisins and let rise in bowl until nearly double in size.

- Heat oil in a deep fat fryer. Dip a tablespoon in the hot oil, then use it to drop dough by tablespoonfuls into the deep fat fryer. Fry both sides until brown and cooked inside. Glaze while hot.

GLAZE
1 box (16 ounce) confectioner's
sugar
¼ cup milk

- Mix powdered sugar and milk. Dip the hot cookies into the glaze and remove with a slotted spoon. Transfer to wax paper to drain.

Hint: Cookies can be rolled in granulated or powdered sugar instead of glazing them.

My Sister's Hamentaschen

Traditional Jewish treat on the Festival of Purim

Bella Davidovich   6 dozen

¾ cup vegetable oil
1 ½ cups sugar
4 eggs
2 teaspoons vanilla extract
3 teaspoons baking powder
½ teaspoon salt
5 ½ cups flour

- Preheat oven to 350 degrees. Grease a large baking sheet.

- In a large bowl, combine oil and sugar, mixing well. Add eggs, one at a time, beating until mixture is light and fluffy. Stir in vanilla.

- Sift dry ingredients together and gradually add to the egg mixture. Knead dough until smooth.

- Roll dough on a floured surface and cut into rounds with a 3-inch cookie cutter. Put a full teaspoonful of filling (recipe below) in the center of each round. Draw up two sides, pull the third side across and pinch the edges together, to form a three-cornered pocket.

- Place cookies on prepared baking sheet and bake for 20 minutes.

PRUNE FILLING
1 pound lekvar
4 tablespoons honey
2 cups walnuts, chopped
1 tablespoon lemon juice

- In a mixing bowl, combine all ingredients thoroughly. Use to fill Hamentaschen cookies. The recipe for lekvar may be found in the Accompaniments division of Applause.

Madame Davidovich, truly a pianist in the grand style, shares a favorite dessert made by her sister. The word Hamentasch, although shaped like a three-cornered hat, really means Hamen's pockets. In this case those pockets are filled with a delicious prune filling.

Puppy Dog Paws

A lovely gift!

Kay Lindsey   4 dozen

2 cups flour
2 ½ cups powdered sugar
½ cup unsweetened cocoa
2 ½ teaspoons baking powder
¼ teaspoon salt
3 ½ ounces unsweetened chocolate, coarsely chopped
3 ½ tablespoons vegetable oil
1 ½ cups light brown sugar, firmly packed
⅓ cup light corn syrup
1 ½ tablespoons vanilla extract
4 large egg whites

- In a large bowl, combine the flour, 1 ½ cups of the powdered sugar, cocoa, baking powder and salt.

- In a saucepan, combine the chocolate and oil and cook over low heat, stirring frequently, until melted and smooth. Do not allow to scorch. Remove from heat and let cool slightly. Stir in the brown sugar, corn syrup and vanilla until well blended.

- Using a whisk, beat the egg whites into the chocolate mixture until all lumps in the sugar mix are dissolved. With a spoon, gently stir the chocolate mixture into the dry ingredients just until smooth. Cover the dough and refrigerate until firm enough to shape into balls, at least 2 ½ hours. The dough can rest for up to 12 hours.

- When ready to bake, preheat oven to 350 degrees. Lightly oil your cookie sheets.

- Use the remaining 1 cup of powdered sugar to dust your hands for handling the dough and coating the cookies. Roll portions of dough into 1-inch balls between your palms. Dredge each ball in the powdered sugar until heavily coated. Place on oiled baking sheets about 1 ½ inches apart.

- Bake 8 to 10 minutes, or until the tops are almost firm when touched. Let cookies cool slightly in the pan, then remove with a spatula. Transfer to wire racks to cool. Tops will crinkle up and resemble the bottom of a puppy's paw.

Hint: These cookies make a nice gift. They can be stored several days in airtight containers.

Pecan Diamonds

Diamonds are still a girl's best friend!

Ava Wheaton   80 diamonds

½ cup butter, well chilled
1 ½ cups flour
½ cup ice water

- Using pastry blender, cut butter into flour until mixture resembles coarse meal. Add water and toss lightly with fork. Gather dough into ball, wrap in plastic, and refrigerate one hour.
- Grease and flour 9x13-inch baking pan, not a cookie sheet.
- Roll dough out on lightly floured surface to about 10x14-inch rectangle.
- Fit into prepared pan; dough will come about halfway up sides. Pierce dough with a fork and chill.
- Preheat oven to 400 degrees.

FILLING
1 ½ cups light brown sugar, firmly packed
1 cup butter
½ cup honey
⅓ cup sugar
1 pound chopped pecans or pecan pieces
½ cup whipping cream

- Bring brown sugar, butter, honey and sugar to boil in heavy saucepan over medium heat, stirring constantly. Boil until thick and dark, about 4 minutes, continuing to stir. Remove from heat. Stir in pecans. Blend in cream. Pour the mixture over dough in the pan.
- Bake in the preheated oven until edges of crust are golden, about 25 minutes. Cool completely.
- Cut into 1-inch strips lengthwise then horizontally to create diamond shapes.
- Serve at room temperature.

Mincemeat Filled Butter Cookies

Leave a box for Santa!

Carol Sue Taylor   4 dozen

1 ½ cups butter, softened
¾ cup sugar
¾ cup packed dark brown sugar
1 egg
4 tablespoons milk
4 ½ cups flour
1 teaspoon baking soda
1 ½ cups prepared mincemeat
2 tablespoons brandy

- Cream butter and sugars. Beat in egg and milk. Stir dry ingredients into the creamed mixture. Wrap and chill the dough at least an hour.

- When ready to bake, preheat oven to 375 degrees.

- On a floured surface, roll half of the dough to approximately ⅛-inch thick. Cut with a 2-inch round cookie cutter and place on an ungreased cookie sheet.

- Mix mincemeat and brandy. Spoon ½ teaspoon of the mixture onto each round.

- Roll the remaining dough to ⅛-inch thick and cut as above. Cut out the centers of each circle (a thimble may be used) and place on top of the first rounds. Seal the edges and bake for 10 to 12 minutes.

For mincemeat lovers!

Carol Sue Taylor, owner of "A Catered Affair" served as a consultant to **Applause**.

Cinnamon Sticks

Anne Skinner   60 to 80 sticks

1　cup butter
¾ cup sugar
2 cups flour
1 egg, divided
4 teaspoons cinnamon
1 teaspoon vanilla extract
1 cup pecans, chopped

- Preheat oven to 350 degrees. Grease a large cookie sheet.

- Cream the butter and sugar. Gradually add the flour, egg yolk, cinnamon and vanilla extract. Place on the cookie sheet and pat down until about ¼ inch thick. This is easier if you cover it with waxed paper and roll out with a rolling pin.

- Beat the egg white slightly and spread over the dough. Press the chopped nuts over the surface and bake about 20 minutes, being careful not to burn. Cut into pieces while hot and cool before removing from pan. These will keep in airtight containers for days!

Apricot Bars

Almeda Hamilton   30 bars

1 cup dried apricots, diced
¾ cup water
1 cup flour
6 tablespoons butter
1 ½ cups brown sugar
1 tablespoon cornstarch
¼ teaspoon salt
2 teaspoons orange peel, grated
2 tablespoons orange juice
2 eggs, beaten
1 ½ cups flaked coconut

- Preheat oven to 350 degrees. Grease a 9x12-inch baking pan.
- Combine apricots and water in a saucepan. Cover and simmer 20 minutes. Watch carefully to avoid burning.
- While the apricots are cooking, mix the flour, butter and ½ cup of the sugar and press into prepared pan. Bake 20 minutes.
- Mix the remaining cup of sugar with the cornstarch and salt. Stir into the undrained apricots and cook until thickened, stirring constantly. Remove from heat and stir in remaining ingredients, reserving a little coconut.
- Spread the apricot mixture over the baked crust. Sprinkle the top with some coconut. Bake 25 minutes. Cool in the pan. Cut into bars.

Hint: Must be refrigerated after cooking. Can be frozen.

199

Lemon Crumb Squares

Marilyn Ehlers   2 dozen

1 can Eagle Brand milk
½ cup lemon juice
1 tablespoon grated lemon rind
1 ½ cup sifted flour
1 tablespoon baking powder
½ tablespoon salt
⅔ cup butter
1 cup dark brown sugar, firmly packed
1 cup uncooked oatmeal

- Preheat oven to 350 degrees. Grease 8x12-inch baking dish.
- Blend together milk, juice, lemon rind and set aside.
- Sift together flour, baking powder, and salt.
- Cream butter and sugar together. Add oatmeal and flour mixture and mix until crumbly. Spread half the mixture in the prepared pan and pat down.
- Spread milk and lemon mixture over the top and cover with the remaining crumb mixture.
- Bake until brown around the edges, about 25 minutes.
- Cool in pan for 15 minutes; cut into 2-inch squares and chill in pan until firm.

Saw Mill Toffee Bars

Betsy White   36 servings

4 tablespoons butter, melted
1 ½ cups graham cracker crumbs
1 ½ cups pecans, chopped
1 ½ cup butter, divided
1 box (16 ounces) confectioner's sugar
3 eggs, lightly beaten
8 ounces unsweetened chocolate, melted and cooled
1 tablespoon Grand Marnier

Hint: This is a large, rich dessert and it's nice to keep some in the freezer for unexpected guests.

- Butter 11x15-inch jelly roll pan.
- Combine melted butter and crumbs and line the bottom of the pan with the mixture. Chill.
- Toast the chopped pecans in ½ cup melted butter.
- Mix 1 cup soft butter, sugar and eggs slowly. Stir in melted chocolate, add toasted pecans and butter. Add Grand Marnier. Spread mixture over crumb crust. Return to the refrigerator until chilled.
- Serve with a dollop of unsweetened whipped cream.

Cheesecake Bars

Carole Almond 48 bars

1 cup flour
¼ cup light brown sugar
1 cup pecans, finely chopped
¼ pound unsalted butter, melted

- Preheat oven to 350 degrees.
- Mix all ingredients in a small bowl. Press into the bottom of a 9x13-inch glass dish. Bake 10 to 15 minutes or until lightly brown. Set aside.

FILLING
2 packages (8 ounce) cream cheese
1 cup sugar
1 teaspoon vanilla extract
3 eggs

- In a medium bowl, beat the cream cheese, sugar and vanilla together. Add the eggs and beat well. Pour over the crust and bake for 20 minutes.

GLAZE
2 cups sour cream
6 tablespoons sugar
1 teaspoon vanilla extract

- In a small bowl, mix the cream, sugar and vanilla. Pour over the baked filling. Return to oven and bake 3 to 5 more minutes. Cool and refrigerate before cutting.

Baked Fudge

Addictive!

Patricia Dickey 9 to 12 servings

4 eggs, beaten
2 cups sugar
1 cup butter
1 cup pecans, broken
4 heaping tablespoons cocoa
4 rounded tablespoons flour
2 teaspoons vanilla extract

This is a quintessential Tulsa recipe, and has been enjoyed by countless patrons of The Garden in Utica Square. Reprinted from The **Tulsa World**.

- Preheat oven to 325 degrees.
- To well beaten eggs, add sugar and butter and beat well again.
- Sift cocoa and flour together. Add broken pecans. Fold into sugar, butter and egg mixture. Add vanilla extract. Pour into 9x12-inch baking dish.
- Set dish in a pan of hot water, enough to come half to one inch up on sides of pan.
- Bake in the oven for 45 minutes to 1 hour. Fudge will have the consistency of firm custard and will be crusty on top
- Serve with a dollop of whipped cream on each piece.

201

Chocolate Pecan Pie Bars

With bourbon, too!

JoAnn Arneson   2 dozen

FIRST LAYER
1 ¼ cups flour
¼ cup sugar
½ teaspoon baking powder
½ teaspoon cinnamon
½ cup butter
1 cup pecans, chopped

- Preheat oven to 350 degrees. Grease a 9x13-inch baking pan.

- Stir flour, sugar, baking powder and cinnamon together. Use a pastry blender to cut the butter into the dry ingredients. The mixture should be the consistency of coarse crumbs. Stir in the finely chopped pecans and pat dough into the bottom of prepared baking pan. Bake 10 minutes.

SECOND LAYER
¼ cup butter
1 square semisweet chocolate
3 eggs, beaten
1 ¼ cups brown sugar
1 teaspoon vanilla extract
2 tablespoons bourbon or water

- Stir butter and chocolate over low heat until chocolate is melted. Combine remaining ingredients and slowly add chocolate mixture, stirring until well blended.

- Pour over the baked crust. Bake an additional 20 minutes or until the filling mixture is firm. Cool and cut into bars to serve.

Cranberry Walnut Pie

Gary Graffman
8 servings

FRENCH PIE CRUST
1 cup flour
6 tablespoons butter
2 tablespoons sugar
1 egg yolk
1 tablespoon cold water
pinch salt

- Preheat oven to 350 degrees.
- Cut butter into flour with pastry cutter or food processor. Use frozen butter with processor. Add remaining ingredients gradually and mix just until ball of dough can be formed. Flatten ball of dough slightly, wrap in plastic, and place in refrigerator for at least one hour.
- Roll out dough quite thin and line a 9-inch pie plate. Cover with plastic and let rest in refrigerator.

FILLING
12 ounces cranberries
1 cup water
3 eggs
1 cup dark corn syrup
1 cup sugar
2 tablespoons butter, melted
1 teaspoon vanilla extract
1 tablespoon rum (optional)
1 cup walnuts, chopped
pinch salt

- Bring 1 cup water to a boil and pour in cranberries, cooking until soft, about 10 minutes. Drain and reserve juice.
- Beat eggs and mix in corn syrup, sugar, melted butter, vanilla, rum and salt. Then add nuts and cooled, cooked cranberries. Pour into unbaked pie crust.
- Bake for 45 to 60 minutes, until set. Cool and chill.

Concert pianist, Gary Graffman, shared this recipe with us after a spectacular performance of the Ravel concerto for the left hand.

When he was not on the outlaw trail making "withdrawals" from banks, Charles Arthur "Pretty Boy" Floyd - - Oklahoma's most famous and beloved bandit - - enjoyed baking apple pies. In 1933, one of "Pretty Boy's" mouth-watering creations even won top honors at a country pie supper where one respected sheriff, unaware of who had done the baking, tasted a slice and declared it the best pie he'd ever put in his mouth.

Michael Wallis, the popular Oklahoma author who has chronicled Route 66, oil barons, BBQ, Native Americans, and so much more in the Sooner State, is the official Floyd biographer. His book, **Pretty Boy: The Life and Times of Charles Arthur Floyd**, earned Wallis one of his trio of Pulitzer Prize nominations.

Wallis points out that during Floyd's thirty years on earth, the Oklahoma bandit baked dozens of pies. This is the best version.

Pretty Boy's Apple Pie

Michael Wallis   6 servings

PIE CRUST
2 cups flour
¾ cup lard
1 teaspoon salt
6-7 tablespoons cold water

APPLE FILLING
1 pound fresh apples, peeled and sliced, or one 16-ounce can
2 tablespoons fresh lemon juice
½ teaspoon ground nutmeg
½ teaspoon ground cinnamon
½ cup white sugar
¼ cup seedless raisins
1 cup brown sugar
2 tablespoons flour
2 tablespoons butter
½ cup shelled Oklahoma pecans
¼ cup milk

- Prepare crust by working the flour, lard and salt together until crumbly. Mix in cold water until dough holds together in big pieces. Divide into two equal balls.

- On a floured surface roll out one ball thin enough to line a 9-inch pie tin. Roll out second ball for the top crust.

- Preheat oven to 450 degrees.

- Prepare the filling by placing the apples in the lined pan. Sprinkle with nutmeg, cinnamon and lemon juice. Spread the white sugar and raisins evenly over the apples.

- Mix the brown sugar, flour and butter in a bowl. When well blended, spread over the contents

Continued on next page

Continued from previous page

of the pie tin and sprinkle with pecans. Add most of the milk and cover with the top crust. Prick top with a fork and brush the rest of the milk on the crust.

- Bake for 10 minutes at 450 degrees, then reduce heat to 350 degrees and bake another 30 minutes until crust is golden.

HARD SAUCE
½ cup butter
1 ½ cups powdered sugar
1 tablespoon boiling water
1 tablespoon brandy or rum (if no "moonshine" available)

- Cream the butter until light. Beat in the sugar and add water.
- Then beat in the liquor and serve on each slice of pie. If you dare, add a scoop of homemade vanilla ice cream.

Pumpkin Chiffon Pie

A delicious Tulsa recipe!

Carol Rowland   6 servings

1 prepared pie crust
1 cup canned pumpkin
1 cup sugar, divided
1 cup milk
1 teaspoon cinnamon
½ teaspoon salt
½ teaspoon ginger
¼ teaspoon nutmeg
2 tablespoons butter, melted
¼ cup cold water
1 envelope Knox gelatin
3 eggs, separated

- Heat pumpkin in top of double boiler for at least 10 minutes, stirring until thick.
- Mix egg yolks, milk, half of the sugar, and add to the pumpkin.
- Then stir in salt, spices and butter, cooking to a custard consistency.
- Remove from heat and add gelatin which has been dissolved in cold water. Chill.
- When mixture begins to stiffen, fold in fluffy, beaten egg whites, to which the balance of sugar has been added.
- Pour into the baked, cooled pie shell and chill thoroughly. Before serving, top each piece with a dollop of whipped cream.

Fresh Strawberry Pie

Karen Casabon   8 servings

3 tablespoons cornstarch
1 cup sugar
1 cup water
3 tablespoons strawberry gelatin
1 quart fresh strawberries
1 9-inch pie crust, baked
1 pint heavy cream, whipped

- Combine the cornstarch, sugar and water and cook, stirring constantly, over very low heat until mixture thickens.
- Remove from heat and add the strawberry gelatin. Stir until gelatin is completely dissolved. Cool.
- Clean strawberries and place on paper towel to dry. When dry, arrange in the baked pie shell. Pour cooled filling over the strawberries and cover with whipped cream.

Sunny Silver Pie

Handed down through three generations!

Mary Hasler   6 servings

½ tablespoon unflavored gelatin
⅓ cup cold water
4 eggs, separated
3 tablespoons lemon juice
zest from ½ lemon
1 cup sugar, divided
⅛ teaspoon salt
1 9-inch pie shell, baked
1 cup whipping cream
3 tablespoons sugar
¼ teaspoon lemon extract

- Place gelatin in cold water to soften.
- In top of double boiler over hot (not boiling) water, whip egg yolks with water, lemon juice, lemon zest, ½ cup sugar and salt. Cook until thickened. Remove double boiler from heat, leaving lemon-egg mixture over the hot water. Add the softened gelatin, mixing well.
- Beat egg whites, adding remaining sugar gradually, until stiff but not dry. Fold egg whites into cooked mixture and pour into pie shell. Cool in refrigerator until set.
- Whip the cream and add sugar and lemon extract. Spread over pie before serving.

206

Okmulgee's Pecan Pie

Glenn Shoaf   12 servings

2 large pastry shells, unbaked
2 ⅔ cups sugar
2 tablespoons butter
¼ teaspoon salt
1 ½ cups corn syrup
7 large eggs, beaten well
1 ½ teaspoons vanilla extract
pecans, to cover bottom of two pie
shells

- Preheat oven to 325 degrees.
- In mixer, blend sugar, butter and salt together until smooth. Add corn syrup to mixture slowly until well mixed. Add eggs to the mixture, one at a time, until well incorporated. Be sure to scrape sides of mixing bowl while adding corn syrup and eggs. Add vanilla extract.
- Place large amount of pecans in the bottom of pie shells. Fill pie shells and bake until medium firm, about 50 minutes.

The World's Largest Pecan Pie, baked in June of 1989, was 40 feet in diameter and weighed 16 ½ tons. The filling was mixed by two new cement trucks. This pie served 22,000 people at the Okmulgee Pecan Festival. Only in Oklahoma!

Sour Cream Pecan Pie

Very rich, but delicious!

Diann Lemons   2 pies

4 egg yolks
2 cups granulated sugar
2 cups sour cream
½ cup flour, sifted
½ teaspoon lemon extract
¼ teaspoon salt
2 9-inch pie crusts, baked
TOPPING
4 egg whites
2 cups brown sugar
2 cups pecans, broken

- Preheat oven to 325 degrees.
- Cook ingredients in a double boiler until thickened, about 45 minutes. Pour into 2 baked pie crusts.
- Beat egg whites until fluffy. Mix in brown sugar then stir in pecans. Spread over the filling.
- Bake 15 minutes or until brown.

Hammett House Lemon Pecan Pie

Colleen Green | 6 servings

3 whole eggs, beaten
⅓ stick butter, melted
1 ½ cups sugar
¾ cup pecan halves
1 teaspoon lemon extract
juice of ½ lemon
1 unbaked pie crust

- Preheat oven to 350 degrees.
- Mix in order given and whip by hand. Do not use an electric mixer.
- Pour into pie crust and bake 10 minutes. Reduce temperature to 300 degrees and bake until the filling is set, about 35 minutes.

Claremore's Hammett House has a long tradition of fine homemade pies. Travelers along Route 66 made this a regular stop.

Pumpkin Pecan Pie

It's a winner!

Thelma Ortner | 6 servings

PUMPKIN LAYER
1 egg
1 cup canned pumpkin
⅓ cup sugar
½ teaspoon cinnamon
¼ teaspoon ginger
⅛ teaspoon cloves
1 9-inch pie shell, unbaked

- Preheat oven to 350 degrees.
- Stir egg, pumpkin, sugar and spices together until well blended. Spread evenly in bottom of pie shell.

PECAN LAYER
2 eggs, beaten
⅔ cup corn syrup
⅔ cup sugar
2 tablespoon butter, melted
½ teaspoon vanilla extract
1 cup pecans

- Mix and spoon carefully over pumpkin layer.
- Bake for 1 hour.

Fudge Pecan Pie

Mary Hasler   8 servings

2 ounces unsweetened chocolate
¼ cup butter
½ cup brown sugar, firmly packed
½ cup sugar
3 eggs, room temperature
¼ teaspoon salt
½ cup half and half cream
¼ cup corn syrup
½ teaspoon vanilla extract
1 cup pecans, chopped
1 9-inch pastry shell
vanilla ice cream or whipped cream

- Preheat oven to 350 degrees.
- Melt chocolate and butter in top of double boiler. Add sugars, stirring until sugar is melted. Add eggs, one at a time, beating well after each addition. Stir in salt, cream, corn syrup and vanilla extract. When well mixed, fold in pecans. Pour into unbaked pie shell.
- Bake 55 minutes or until set. Cool at room temperature.
- May be served warm with vanilla ice cream or chilled with whipped cream.

Dottie's Chocolate Pie

Jeannie Drake   8 servings

1 ½ cups sugar
3 tablespoons Hershey's cocoa
½ cup butter, melted
3 eggs, slightly beaten
1 can (5 ounce) evaporated milk
1 teaspoon vanilla extract
1 prepared pie shell
confectioner's sugar

- Preheat oven to 350 degrees.
- Mix the sugar and cocoa and add to the melted butter. Fold in the eggs, milk and vanilla.
- Pour into the unbaked pie shell and bake for 35 minutes or until a knife inserted comes out clean. Sprinkle with powdered sugar when cool. Delicious served with whipped cream.

Frozen Peanut Pie

Your family will like it!

Ruth Ralston   8 servings

4 ounces cream cheese, softened
1 cup confectioner's sugar
½ cup creamy peanut butter
½ cup milk
1 carton (9 ounce) Cool Whip topping
1 9-inch graham cracker crust, baked and cooled
¼ cup salted peanuts, finely chopped

- Whip cheese until soft and fluffy. Beat in sugar and peanut butter. Slowly add milk, blending thoroughly into mixture. Fold in Cool Whip. Pour into baked pie shell.

- Sprinkle with chopped peanuts. Freeze until firm and serve. Wrap in plastic after completely frozen. Cut pieces as you need them and return to the freezer.

Pumpkin Ice Cream Pie

Kay Lindsey   8 servings

40 gingersnaps
1 heaping tablespoon sugar
6 teaspoons butter, melted
1 ½ cups canned pumpkin
½ cup sugar
1 teaspoon ginger
1 teaspoon cinnamon
½ teaspoon nutmeg
3 cups vanilla ice cream
2 8-inch pie plates (or 1-10 inch pie plate)

- Preheat oven to 300 degrees.

- Break gingersnaps into pieces. Combine with sugar in food processor and use metal blade to chop finely, 30 seconds. Add butter and pulse about 6 times to blend. Press firmly into pie pan.

- Bake until set, about 12 minutes.

- In the food processor, combine pumpkin, sugar and spices. Add ice cream, pulsing several times until smooth. Pour into cooled pie shell and freeze until firm. Before serving, let stand at room temperature until soft enough to cut. Garnish with whipped cream.

Bananas Foster Pie

It's waiting for you in the freezer!

Colleen Blaylock Green   6 to 8 servings

1 graham cracker crust
2 quarts almond praline or butter
pecan ice cream, softened
¼ cup butter
½ cup brown sugar
¼ teaspoon cinnamon
¼ cup dark rum
6 bananas, peeled and sliced

- Spread ice cream evenly in the pie crust. Freeze.

- When ready to serve, melt the butter in a skillet and blend in the brown sugar, cinnamon and rum. Add the sliced bananas and heat thoroughly.

- Cut pie into serving pieces and top each piece with the warm topping. Serve immediately.

This delicious ice cream pie is from **The Aunt's Cookbook** which was edited by Colleen, an Editor of **Applause**.

211

Fruit Yogurt Pie

Marion DeVore   8 servings

HONEY GRAHAM CRACKER CRUST
1 ½ cups of graham cracker crumbs
2 tablespoons honey
1 tablespoon vegetable oil

- Preheat oven to 350 degrees.
- Blend graham cracker crumbs, honey and oil and mix well. Pat into a 9-inch pie pan. Bake for 10 minutes. Cool.

FILLING
1 ½ cups plain nonfat yogurt
1 ½ cups nonfat cottage cheese, drained
4 tablespoons honey
1 teaspoon vanilla extract, or use Cointreau, Creme de Menthe, or Amaretto
¼ teaspoon fresh lemon juice
1 envelope unflavored gelatin
Fruit of your choice: peaches, strawberries, etc.

- Combine yogurt, cottage cheese, honey, lemon juice and the flavor of your choice in blender.
- While blender is running, dissolve gelatin by first stirring in one tablespoon cold water, then three tablespoons boiling water. Add the dissolved gelatin to the blender and blend well.
- Place the fresh fruit in the pie shell and pour the yogurt mixture over it. You can reverse this procedure if you wish. Chill until set.

Marion DeVore and Frank Ratka, Symphony Manager at the time, spearheaded the first Oklahoma City Arts Festival which has grown to be one of the top ten Arts Festivals in the United States.

Peach Cobbler

Orene Walters   8 servings

CRUST
3 cups flour
1 teaspoon salt
1 cup shortening
¾ cup ice water

- Preheat oven to 350 degrees.
- Prepare crust by mixing flour and salt in a bowl. Cut the shortening into the flour mix mixture until it looks like cornmeal. Add water gradually, cutting in with knives. Do not knead. Form into 2 balls and roll out on floured board. Fit one circle into pie tin. Cut the rest into 1-inch strips.

COBBLER
1 quart of fresh sliced peaches
¼ cup water, if needed
1 cup sugar
1 teaspoon of cinnamon
1 tablespoon cornstarch or flour

- Put peaches into a saucepan. Mix the dry ingredients and pour over the peaches. Bring to a boil over low heat. Watch closely to prevent sticking.
- Pour peaches into a baking dish and cover the top with strips of the dough, crisscrossing. Crimp the edges to hold the dough in place and sprinkle the top with sugar and dabs of butter.
- Bake for 40 minutes or until light brown on top.

Orene Walters is a six time Grand Champion Cobbler winner at the annual Peach Festival held in Porter, the Peach Capital of Oklahoma. The Porter area boasts over 50,000 peach trees with over 40 different varieties. People come from miles around to sample this wonderful fruit.

Frozen Fresh Lemon Tarts

Kay Floyd   12 servings

3 eggs, separated
¼ cup fresh lemon juice
⅔ cup sugar
¼ teaspoon salt
1 teaspoon lemon zest, grated
1 teaspoon vanilla extract
1 cup cream, whipped
½ cup pecans, ground

- In double boiler, combine well beaten egg yolks, lemon juice, sugar and salt. Cook over hot, not boiling, water until custard coats spoon, stirring often, about 5 minutes. Chill. Stir in lemon zest and vanilla.

- Beat egg whites until stiff. Fold gently into custard. Fold in whipped cream.

- Place 12 fluted baking cups in muffin tin. Sprinkle bottom of each with 1 teaspoon ground nuts. Fill with lemon mixture. Sprinkle remaining nuts over the top.

- Freeze 5 to 6 hours or overnight. Remove a few minutes before serving.

Bourbon Sweet Potato Pie

Came to Oklahoma in a covered wagon!

Diann Lemons   12 servings

1 teaspoon baking soda
1 ½ cups sugar
8 cups sweet potatoes, cooked and mashed
½ cup butter, melted
4 egg yolks, beaten
1 cup milk
1 cup bourbon
1 cup pecans (optional)
meringue topping

- Preheat oven to 325 degrees.

- In a large bowl, whisk the baking soda into the sugar. Add the sweet potatoes and stir well.

- Add the melted butter, the egg yolks, and then the liquids, stirring well after each addition.

- Add the pecans and pour into a baking dish. There is no crust! Bake 30 minutes.

- Top with a meringue, using these left-over egg whites. See recipe page 241.

Baked Pear Elegance

Eleanor Hill   8 servings

4 fresh pears, cored and halved
¼ cup pineapple-apricot jam
2 tablespoons melted butter
2 tablespoons brown sugar
2 tablespoons sherry
1 tablespoon lemon juice
dash of salt
¼ cup corn flake crumbs

- Preheat oven to 325 degrees. Butter a 9x13-inch baking pan.
- Arrange pears in prepared dish and spread with jam.
- Combine butter, brown sugar, sherry, lemon and salt; spoon mixture over pears. Sprinkle with crumbs and bake for 20 to 25 minutes, basting from time to time. Serve warm.

Calories per serving: 124
Saturated Fat 2 g
Cholesterol 8 mg
Total Fat 3 g (23% of Calories)
Sodium 91 mg

Lemon Sponge Cups

Nancy King   6 servings

2 tablespoons butter, softened
1 cup sugar
5 tablespoons flour
¼ teaspoon salt
5 tablespoons lemon juice
1 lemon, grated rind only
3 eggs, separated
1 ½ cups milk

- Preheat oven to 350 degrees.
- Cream butter. Add the sugar, flour, salt, lemon juice and lemon rind. Whisk the egg yolks into the milk and add this mixture to the batter. Fold in the stiffly beaten egg whites. Pour into greased custard cups. Set the cups in a pan of water and bake 45 minutes. When done, each cup will contain lemon custard at the bottom of the cup and sponge cake on the top. Cool. Unmold. Garnish with lemon zest curls and maraschino cherries.

Hint: When grating the lemon rind, avoid grating the white portion. It will add an undesirable bitter flavor.

215

Royal Syllabub

Martha Lou Findeiss   4 servings

2 egg whites
4 ounces caster sugar
juice of ½ lemon
½ cup sweet white wine
1 cup whipping cream

- Beat egg whites to stiff peak stage. Fold in sugar, lemon juice and wine.

- Beat cream until it holds its shape then fold into egg white mixture.

- Spoon into parfait glasses or champagne flutes. Refrigerate 4 hours or overnight.

- Use small spoons, not dessert spoons. Could be accompanied by a bar or cookie.

Martha is London's connection to Oklahoma City! Caster sugar is a finer grind of sugar used in England. Regular sugar may be substituted.

Strawberries Newport

Yvette Fleckinger   6 servings

1 box frozen puff pastry shells
1 recipe French Custard Filling
(omit vanilla flavoring)
1 tablespoon Amaretto
1 quart fresh strawberries, sliced
6 whole berries for garnish
2 tablespoons confectioner's sugar
2 cups whipping cream, whipped

- Bake pastry shells according to package directions. Remove lids and hollow out the inside.

- Sprinkle confectioner's sugar over strawberries. Refrigerate until ready to serve.

- When ready to serve, stir Amaretto into the custard. Fill shells with custard. Place a large scoop of sliced strawberries on top of custard. Top with a generous serving of whipped cream. Garnish with a whole berry.

An adaptation of Oklahoma's favorite festival dessert from the annual Oklahoma City Arts Festival, originally served at the Newport Restaurant.

Cream Puffs

Chicken salad inside and it's lunch!

Aileen Frank   8 to 12 shells

1 cup boiling water
½ cup butter
½ teaspoon salt
1 cup flour
4 eggs

- Preheat oven to 400 degrees.
- Combine water, butter and salt and bring to a boil. Add flour and beat briskly with a wooden spoon until mixture leaves the side of the pan and no longer clings to the spoon. Remove from heat and cool slightly. Add eggs one at a time, beating thoroughly after each addition until the mixture is smooth.
- Drop by teaspoonfuls for small puffs or tablespoonfuls for large puffs onto a well greased baking sheet. Shape the spoonfuls into rounds as you drop them, piling slightly in the middle.
- Bake for 30 minutes. Lower heat to 350 degrees and continue to bake for 10 minutes.
- To serve, cut a slit in the side of each puff and fill with French Custard Filling.

French Custard Filling

Colleen Blaylock Green   2 cups

⅓ cup sugar
1 tablespoon flour
1 tablespoon cornstarch
¼ teaspoon salt
1 ½ cups milk
1 egg yolk, beaten
1 teaspoon vanilla extract
½ cup heavy cream, whipped

- Mix first four ingredients in a saucepan. Stir in the milk and cook, stirring, until thickened. Cook 2 to 3 minutes longer. Whip some of the hot mixture into the egg yolks then return this to the hot mixture, stirring constantly, for a few more minutes. Remove from heat and add vanilla extract. Let cool, then beat until smooth and add the whipped cream.

217

Maple Nut Mousse

Ethel Findlay   6 servings

2 eggs, beaten
¾ cup maple syrup
½ cup pecans
1 cup heavy cream

- Heat the syrup and pour into the beaten eggs while beating. Cook in a double boiler until thick. Cool.
- Whip the cream. Fold the whipped cream and nuts into the egg mixture. Chill and serve.

Mighty Mousse
Mighty good!

Kay Floyd   12 servings

1 cup walnuts
2 tablespoons unflavored gelatin
½ cup cold water
5 eggs, separated
½ cup brown sugar, firmly packed
2 tablespoons instant coffee
¼ teaspoon salt
1 cup milk, scalded
¼ to ½ cup dark rum
18 unfilled split ladyfingers
¾ cup sugar
1 teaspoon vanilla extract
1 cup heavy cream, whipped

- Preheat oven to 350 degrees. Drop walnuts into boiling water and cook 3 minutes. Drain.
- Spread the nuts in a shallow pan and bake for 15 minutes, stirring several times. Watch that nuts do not burn.
- Soften gelatin in cold water. Beat yolks in top of double boiler, stir in brown sugar, coffee and salt; gradually blend in milk. Cook over boiling water, stirring constantly for 5 minutes, or until thickened.
- Remove custard mixture from heat, add dissolved gelatin and stir until smooth.
- Blend in rum. Chill until thick, but not set.
- Line sides and bottom of 9-inch springform pan with ladyfingers. Beat egg whites until fluffy, add vanilla and beat in sugar one tablespoon at a time to make a stiff meringue.
- Fold walnuts, custard and whipped cream into the meringue. Chill several hours or overnight. Remove sides of pan and serve.

Coconut Mousse

Susan Robinson   10 servings

1 pint half and half cream
3 tablespoons unflavored gelatin
⅓ cup water
1 cup sugar
2 cups fresh grated coconut
1 teaspoon almond extract
1 ½ pints whipping cream

- Soak gelatin in the water until dissolved.
- In a saucepan heat half and half to a boil. Add gelatin mixture and sugar, stirring until dissolved. Cool and add coconut.
- In a bowl, beat whipping cream with almond extract until stiff. Fold into coconut mixture and pour mousse into an 8-cup mold. Chill the mousse until firm.

Kahlua Mousse

Jo Russell   6 to 8 servings

½ cup sugar
⅓ cup water
4 eggs
pinch salt
1 package (6 ounce) chocolate chips
3 tablespoons Kahlua
2 tablespoons Cognac or brandy
2 cups whipping cream, chilled

- Mix water and sugar and heat slowly until dissolved. Boil for 5 minutes but do not allow to crystallize.
- Place eggs, salt and chocolate chips in blender and process until smooth.
- Add sugar syrup in a slow stream as you blend on medium speed. Mix until smooth. Cool slightly.
- Add Kahlua and Cognac and blend.
- Place in a bowl and chill in refrigerator until almost stiff.
- Beat whipping cream until it forms peaks. Stir ¾ of the whipped cream into chocolate mixture with wire whisk. Reserve remainder for garnish.
- Serve in small pots de créme cups.

Elegant Daiquiri Soufflé

A beautiful dessert!

George Seminoff   12 servings

½ cup light rum
2 tablespoons unflavored gelatin
10 eggs, separated
2 cups sugar, divided
½ cup lemon juice
½ cup lime juice
grated rind of 2 lemons and 2 limes
⅛ teaspoon salt
3 cups whipping cream, divided
crystallized violets (optional)
1 package (2 ounce) pistachio nuts, finely chopped

- Cut a piece of aluminum foil to fit around a 1 ½-quart soufflé dish, allowing a 1-inch overlap. Fold the paper in half and wrap around the dish with the foil extending 5 inches above the rim of the dish to form a collar. Set aside.

- Combine light rum and gelatin. Let stand five minutes. Meanwhile, beat the egg yolks until light and fluffy. Gradually add one cup of the sugar, beating constantly until thick and lemon colored. Combine the yolk mix with the fruit juices, grated rind and salt in a 2 ½-quart saucepan. Cook over low heat, stirring constantly until thickened (about 12 minutes). Remove from the heat and add the gelatin mixture, stirring until dissolved. Allow to cool.

- In a large chilled mixer bowl, beat the egg whites until stiff peaks form, gradually adding ½ cup of the sugar. Beat two cups of the whipping cream with ¼ cup of sugar until stiff peaks form. Fold the whipping cream and egg whites into the cooled yolk mix and pour into the soufflé dish. Chill until firm. Soufflé may be frozen.

- Remove the collar and gently pat crushed nuts on the exposed sides of the soufflé. Whip the remaining one cup of cream with ¼ cup sugar until stiff peaks form. Spoon in mounds on top of the soufflé or fill a pastry bag and decorate the top with rosettes and petals. Garnish with crystallized violets and twisted slices of lime if desired. Soufflé may be frozen.

When **Southern Living** was preparing an article about George and Sharon's home, this luscious dessert was served after an omelet party. The magazine guests asked for and printed the recipe. This will be a favorite in your home, too.

Curried Fruit A Cappella

Sings with spice!

Carol Crawford   8 servings

**Peaches, pears, apricots,
pineapple, cherries
½ cup butter
2 teaspoons curry powder
1 cup brown sugar
whipped cream, optional**

- You need enough fruit, cut into bite-size pieces, to fill a medium size square casserole.
- Melt butter and mix in curry powder and sugar. Stir into fruit and marinate about 2 hours.
- Bake at 350 degrees for ½ hour.
- Serve warm with a dollop of whipped cream if you wish accompaniment.

Ms. Crawford serves as Artistic Director of Tulsa Opera which enjoys a national reputation for artistic excellence and sound management. Under the company's education program, each year thousands of children are introduced to opera.

Grand Marnier Yogurt

Glenna Boyd   4 servings

**1 pint frozen, nonfat vanilla
yogurt
1 teaspoon pure vanilla extract
1 tablespoon Grand Marnier liquer**

- Place the frozen yogurt in a bowl and stir, stir, stir until you have removed all the air.
- Add vanilla extract and liquer and refreeze.
- Spoon into stemmed dessert glasses and serve with dainty, crisp cookies.

Calories per serving: 127
Saturated Fat 0 g
Cholesterol 0 mg
Total Fat 0 g (0% of Calories)
Sodium 97 mg

Bride's Bread Pudding

Your next family favorite!

Lynn Kelly   8 servings

1 loaf (10 oz.) stale French bread
2 tablespoons water
2 ¼ cups evaporated milk
7 eggs, beaten
1 can Eagle Brand milk
½ cup sugar
½ cup raisins
1 can (8 oz.) pineapple, crushed
2 tablespoons vanilla extract
¼ cup butter, melted

- Preheat oven to 350 degrees. Lightly coat 9x12-inch baking dish with cooking spray.
- Tear bread into pieces and sprinkle lightly with water.
- Blend in all other ingredients.
- Prepare a large pan of water and place on middle rack in oven.
- Fill baking dish with pudding and place in water pan. Bake for one hour or until set.
- Serve warm with Bourbon Sauce.

BOURBON SAUCE
1 cup butter
2 cups super fine granulated sugar
nutmeg to taste
½ cup bourbon

- Using an electric mixer, combine sugar and butter until light and fluffy.
- Add nutmeg and bourbon, beating until smooth. Sugar should be completely dissolved.
- Place a small scoop of sauce on top of warm pudding and serve immediately.

As a young bride, Lynn brought this pudding recipe to our state. Oklahomans agree this is the most delicious bread pudding recipe in the Southwest.

Flan Joel

Joel Levine   8 servings

CARAMEL
⅓ cup sugar
⅓ cup water

- Place the sugar on the bottom of a round fluted metal baking mold (8 ½ x 3 ½ inches.) Add water.
- Place the mold on high heat and bring mixture to a boil. Watch carefully until it reaches an amber color. Remove immediately from heat to prevent burning.
- Swish from side to side to coat the entire mold with the caramel. Be careful not to burn yourself doing this!

FLAN MIXTURE
3 cups milk or half & half cream
6 eggs
6 tablespoons sugar
1 teaspoon vanilla extract

- Preheat oven to 325 degrees.
- Beat the eggs as for an omelette (do not overbeat).
- Heat milk to lukewarm temperature. While beating eggs, gradually add the warm milk. Continue stirring, then gradually add the sugar, sprinkling in one spoon at a time. Mix in the vanilla extract.
- Pour mixture into the caramel lined mold and bake 50 to 55 minutes, until it reaches the consistency of a custard (very slightly brown on top).
- Refrigerate for several hours or overnight.
- Dip in very hot water and unmold on serving platter.

Joel Levine, founder and conductor of the Oklahoma City Philharmonic, shares with us his favorite dessert, originally served by his aunt in France. Mr. Levine is deserving of great applause for the tenacity, the courage and enthusiasm which led to establishing the Oklahoma City Philharmonic, thus continuing a symphonic tradition begun in 1924 in Oklahoma.

Date Pudding

" A favorite of my Norwegian grandmother."

Mex Frates   8 servings

1 package (8 ounce) dates, coarsely
chopped
1 cup English walnuts, chopped
5 eggs, beaten
1 cup sugar
1 cup fresh bread crumbs
½ teaspoon baking powder
pinch salt

- Preheat oven to 300 degrees.
- Mix ingredients together. Butter an 8x8-inch baking dish.
- Pour into the prepared dish. Place dish in a larger pan of hot water and bake for one hour.
- Serve hot with plain or whipped cream.

Dvorsky's Dirt

George Dvorsky   8 to 10 servings

1 package (16 ounces) Oreo cookies
1 package (8 ounce) cream cheese,
softened
2 packages (3 ounce) vanilla
instant pudding
1 carton (12 ounce) Cool Whip
2 ½ cups milk

- Crush cookies in blender.
- Blend together Cool Whip, cream cheese, instant pudding and milk.
- Layer with cookie crumbs in a serving bowl and chill for at least one hour.

It's a hit at every cast party. Being a dessert junkie, this is the best! It's also fun to put it in a real flower pot with artificial flowers and use as a centerpiece at dinner. Serve it with an actual spade!

Yogurt Crepes

Marion DeVore   12 crepes

1 egg or egg substitute
¼ cup warm milk
2 tablespoons butter, melted
½ cup nonfat yogurt
½ cup flour
½ teaspoon baking powder

Calories per serving: 50
Saturated Fat 1 g
Cholesterol 24 mg
Total Fat 3 g (46% of Calories)
Sodium 49 mg

- In a mixing bowl, beat the egg until light, gradually beating in the milk, melted butter and yogurt. Add the dry ingredients to the bowl, mixing until smooth and full of bubbles. Refrigerate for at least three hours. The batter should be the consistency of thick cream.

- Heat a 6-inch skillet or crepe pan, brushed lightly with oil or coated with vegetable spray. Repeated oiling is not necessary. Pour about two tablespoons of batter into the pan all at once. Rotate the pan so the batter will cover the bottom evenly. When the batter is lightly browned on one side, lift it by the edge and turn it over. Cook a few seconds or until it is flecked with brown. Place the crepe on a paper towel. Continue to cook and stack crepes.

- To serve, fill and top with your favorite fruit or sauce.

Cranberry Ice
A family holiday tradition

Karen Mayfield   8 servings

4 cups cranberries
3 cups water
3 cups sugar
Juice of 2 oranges
Juice of 2 lemons

Calories per serving: 337
Saturated Fat 0 g
Cholesterol 0 mg
Total Fat 0 g (0% of Calories)
Sodium 2 mg

- Cook first three ingredients until berries are soft. Press through a sieve and discard solids.
- Add juices and stir to mix well.
- Pour into 9x13-inch glass baking dish and freeze. Stir twice during freezing time. To serve, spoon into glass sherbets.

Buttermilk Ice Cream
Try it! You'll like it!

Garline J. Wheatley   6 servings

3 cups chilled buttermilk
1 can (20 ounce) crushed pineapple
1 cup sugar
1 ½ teaspoons vanilla extract
dash of salt

- Mix all the ingredients. Chill and freeze in ice cream freezer according to manufacturer's direction.

Calories per serving: 184
Saturated Fat 1 g
Cholesterol 3 mg
Total Fat 1 g (4% of Calories)
Sodium 145 mg

Chocolate Truffles

Phyllis Murray   30 truffles

1 package (6 ounce) chocolate chips
½ cup unsalted butter (no substitution)
¾ cup sifted confectioner's sugar
2 egg yolks
2 tablespoons strong coffee
2 tablespoons brandy or rum

- Melt chocolate in a double boiler. Add butter, sugar, brandy, coffee and the egg yolks. Mix together until smooth and creamy.
- The next day, make balls and roll in Nestlés Quick powdered chocolate. Candy will keep in the freezer for several weeks and in the refrigerator for several days. The recipe may be doubled.

Bourbon Candy

Mitzie Lilly   1 ½ pounds

Butter
1 box confectioner's sugar
⅓ cup bourbon
3 cups pecan halves
1 package (8 ounce) chocolate chips

- Cream ¼ cup butter. Gradually add sugar alternately with the bourbon, beating until thick and smooth.
- Chill. Shape half-teaspoonfuls of mixture into small balls, using sugar on hands if needed.
- Press a pecan half on each side of ball and chill.
- Melt chocolate and 1 ½ teaspoons butter over hot water. Dip one end of each candy in the chocolate and place on cookie sheet covered with waxed paper.
- Chill until firm. Add more butter to chocolate mixture if it thickens too much.

Pecan Rolls

Save a bite for Santa!

Patsy Sallee   5 pecan rolls

1 jar (7 ounce) marshmallow cream
1 package (16 ounce)
confectioner's sugar
1 teaspoon vanilla extract
1 package (14 ounce) assorted
vanilla and chocolate caramels
3 tablespoons water
2 ½ cups chopped pecans

- Using your hands, mix the marshmallow cream, vanilla extract and most of the confectioner's sugar. The mixture should be dry. Mix in remaining sugar, if needed.
- Shape mixture into five 4x1-inch rolls. Chill 2 to 3 hours or overnight.
- Combine caramels and water in top of a double boiler and heat until melted. Dip rolls into melted caramels and quickly roll each in pecans. Chill one hour. Cut into slices to serve.

Apricot Delights

Sharon Hodder   1 ½ pounds

1 pound dried apricots, ground
½ cup nutmeats, broken
¾ cup Eagle Brand Milk
coconut

- Mix the ground apricots, nutmeats and milk together and roll into balls.
- Roll the apricot balls in the coconut to coat.
- Place in the refrigerator for several hours or overnight.

Date Balls

Adeanya Hunt   2 dozen

½ cup butter
⅔ cup sugar
2 egg yolks, beaten
1 package (8 ounce) dates, seeded
and chopped
1 cup nuts, chopped
1 cup crisp rice cereal
1 teaspoon vanilla extract

- In a saucepan, melt butter and add sugar, egg yolks and dates. Bring to a boil and boil two minutes, stirring constantly. Remove from heat and add the remaining ingredients. Form the mixture into 1 ½-inch balls.

Peanut Brittle

Ted Wheaton   1 pound

1 pound raw Spanish peanuts
3 cups sugar
butter

- Butter a marble slab if you have one, or a large cookie sheet.

- Place sugar in a large, heavy bottomed skillet. Slowly melt the sugar over medium heat, stirring constantly and frequently scraping the sides of the pan to assure that no unmelted sugar remains. Adjust the heat if necessary to prevent overbrowning. When completely melted, the syrup should be a light caramel color.

- Add the peanuts all at once, stirring quickly until they are distributed evenly and fully coated.

- Pour the candy onto the marble or cookie sheet working quickly to spread it evenly. A second pair of hands to spread the candy is very helpful.

- Allow the candy to cool, then break into pieces and store uncovered. This candy may become sticky if stored in a sealed container or in high humidity.

This old fashioned peanut brittle recipe has been in my family for almost 100 years. An older sister tells the story, "In the small town where the family lived at the turn of the century, early in the holiday season each year an itinerant "candy maker" came for a few days to make the family Christmas treats. He arrived in his colorful cart with copper pots gleaming and fat sacks of sugar and nuts to work his magic with these simple ingredients. Patiently tolerating excited children full of questions and begging for samples, he made the old fashioned candies...taffy, fudge, divinity, and the peanut brittle above." It is a special treat for anyone who enjoys this timeless holiday confection.

Almond Toffee

Dixie Gordon   Two pounds

1 pound butter
1 cup sugar
1 tablespoon light corn syrup
3 tablespoons hot water
1 cup almonds, blanched and toasted
1 package (8 ounce) chocolate chips
½ block of paraffin
¼ cup almonds, blanched, toasted and chopped for garnish

- Combine first 4 ingredients in a large heavy pot. Cook and stir over low heat until mixture registers 290 degrees on a candy thermometer.
- Add nuts and pour on buttered cookie sheets. Spread thin.
- Melt chocolate chips and paraffin together and pour over the first mixture, spreading evenly to cover.
- Sprinkle with chopped almonds to garnish. Cool and break into pieces.

Divine Pecan Turtles

Sinfully good!

Pat Higgins   60 pieces

12 ounces semi-sweet baking chocolate
2 tablespoons vegetable shortening
1 package (14 ounce) caramels
5 tablespoons butter
2 tablespoons milk
1 cup pecans, toasted and chopped
1 teaspoon maple flavoring

- Microwave chocolate and shortening in a 2-quart bowl for 2 to 3 minutes at medium high temperature. Stir.
- Pour half of the melted chocolate mixture into a foil-lined, buttered 9-inch square pan. Refrigerate for 15 minutes.
- Meanwhile, microwave caramels, butter and milk in a 1-quart bowl for 4 to 5 minutes at medium high temperature, stirring occasionally. Stir in pecans and maple flavoring. Pour over refrigerated chocolate layer.
- Reheat remaining chocolate for 1 minute at medium high. Spread over caramel layer. Refrigerate for 2 hours.
- Invert pan on cutting surface. Peel off foil and cut into small squares. Store in the refrigerator. Candy will become sticky if held at room temperature longer than one hour.

Aunt Bill's Brown Candy

Originally called Oklahoma Brown Candy

Jayne Jayroe   6 pounds

6 cups white sugar
2 cups cream
½ cup butter
¼ teaspoon soda
1 tablespoon vanilla extract
2 cups pecans, coarsely chopped or broken

- Place two cups of the sugar in a heavy iron skillet and heat over a low fire. Stir with a wooden spoon to prevent the sugar from scorching. Sugar should be a light brown syrup when finished.

- Meanwhile, pour the other 4 cups of sugar into a deep heavy kettle, add cream and cook slowly over a low fire, stirring to dissolve sugar only until it boils.

- As soon as the sugar in the skillet is melted, pour it into the kettle of boiling sugar and cream in a very fine stream, stirring constantly.

- Continue cooking and stirring until the mixture forms a firm ball (248 degrees) when tested in cold water.

- Remove from heat and immediately add soda, stirring vigorously as it foams up. Add butter, allowing it to melt as you stir. Cool about 10 minutes at room temperature.

- Add vanilla and begin beating. An electric mixer may be used until it gets thick. Continue beating with a wooden spoon until thick and heavy, until glossy look becomes dull.

- Add nuts and mix thoroughly. Pour into buttered pan and cut into squares when slightly cooled.

Oklahoma's first Miss America reminisced about this recipe, "This is not only a sinful, wonderful, fat laden treat, it is also a delightful tradition in our family during the Christmas holiday. The recipe really requires two people...one to pour and one to stir...a kitchen full of family love and warmth. No wonder we have such fond memories of brown candy."

January Thaw

Alice Dotter   1 pound

2 cups sugar
1 cup milk
½ cup white Karo
1 teaspoon soda
1 teaspoon vanilla extract
1 cup pecans
1 tablespoon butter

- Place sugar, milk and Karo in a large heavy pan. Cook over low heat until it boils then stir in soda. Cook until it forms a firm soft ball in cold water (at least 238 degrees) and is a golden brown color. Don't undercook.
- Remove from heat and add pecans, vanilla and butter. Cool 10 minutes and beat until firm. Pour in a buttered pan (6x9-inch) and let cool before cutting.

Christmas Cinnamon Candy

Yvonne Nichols   40 to 50 pieces

1 can (12 ounce) evaporated milk
2 cups sugar
½ cup butter
1 cup pecans, chopped
ground cinnamon

- Place milk, sugar and butter in a heavy sauce pan and cook over low heat, stirring constantly. When mixture boils, stop stirring and cook until mixture reaches 238 degrees on a candy thermometer (soft ball stage).
- Remove pan from heat and stir in pecans.
- While it's warm, pour candy mixture onto waxed paper and roll into a log about 14 inches long. Dust the log with cinnamon until well coated.
- Transfer the candy log to a clean cutting surface and cut in thin slices. Store on a plate in refrigerator.

This recipe was a favorite of Yvonne's mother, Vinita Cravens, who brought many Broadway shows to Oklahoma to great Applause! Every Christmas, Vinita air-expressed this candy to New York producers and to favorite stars, such as Carol Channing, who had performed in Oklahoma many times.

ACCOMPANIMENTS

ACCOMPANIMENTS

Main Dish

Salad

Dessert

QUARTZ MOUNTAIN

Nestled in the rugged granite hills of Southwestern Oklahoma is Quartz Mountain, a magical place. Once the sacred grounds of the Kiowa and Comanche Indians, today it is the site of the Summer Arts Institute. Musicians, artists and writers gain inspiration from nature's palette of wildflowers, grasses, caves and wildlife. Young people, who come from all over Oklahoma and beyond to study with famous artists and writers, leave at the end of summer inspired by the magic of Quartz Mountain.

Microwave Mushroom Sauce
From the Lone Creek Mushroom Farm

Sandra Williams   1 ¼ cups

2 tablespoons butter
¼ pound shiitake mushrooms,
chopped
¼ cup onion, finely chopped
2 tablespoons flour
1 cube chicken bouillon, dissolved
in ¾ cup hot water
1 tablespoon dry sherry
white pepper and ground nutmeg
to taste

- Place butter in 1-quart casserole. Microwave on high to melt. Stir in mushrooms and onion.
- Microwave, covered with waxed paper for 2 minutes. Stir and resume cooking for 1 more minute.
- Stir in flour and microwave, uncovered, for another 30 seconds.
- Gradually mix in the liquid bouillon. Microwave uncovered for 1 minute, then stir several times until mixture has cooked for 3 ½ to 4 minutes.
- Add sherry and pepper and sprinkle with nutmeg.
- Correct seasonings to taste, then cover with waxed paper and let the flavors blend for about 3 minutes.

Encore Bearnaise Sauce
Essential to beef fondue.

Myles Criss   2 cups

6 green onions, minced
2 tablespoons butter
4 egg yolks
¼ cup white wine vinegar
2 teaspoons dried tarragon
¼ teaspoon dry mustard
¼ teaspoon salt
4 drops Tabasco
2 cups butter, melted

- Sauté onions lightly in a little butter and put them in a blender. Add the eggs and spices and mix at medium speed 2 minutes.
- Gradually add melted butter while mixing until all is absorbed. Refrigerate. Allow to soften to serve. Yes, it holds together!

Myles Criss was the founder and first Musical Director of the Canterbury Choral Society. He now directs a festival choir in Topeka.

Apple Chutney

Evelyn Janeway   3 to 4 pints

2 orange rinds
8 cups apples, chopped
4 cups sugar
2 cups raisins
½ cup cider vinegar
¼ teaspoon allspice

- Remove most of white membrane from orange rind, and cut the rind into slivers.
- Combine all ingredients and simmer, uncovered, for 1 hour and 15 minutes (until liquid is reduced and apples are tan in color).

Hint: May be refrigerated in a covered container indefinitely or may be spooned into hot, sterilized canning jars immediately and sealed for storage in the cupboard.

Hint: Good as accompaniment to curry or poultry.

Apricot Onion Chutney

Evelyn Janeway   a scant quart

2 cups dried apricots, washed and quartered
2 tablespoons ginger, cut coarsely
1 cup golden, seedless raisins
½ lemon, thinly sliced and quartered
1 cup onions, sliced thin and halved
1 ½ cups dark brown sugar
½ cup wine vinegar
2 cloves garlic, crushed
1 ½ teaspoons dry mustard
½ teaspoon Tabasco
½ cup tomato juice
½ teaspoon each of salt, cinnamon, cloves and allspice

- Blend all ingredients in order listed. Simmer over low heat until thick, approximately 30 to 45 minutes.
- Pour into small glass containers and seal.

Hint: This is a wonderful accompaniment for meats, as well as served with peach halves topped with a bit of brown sugar and broiled until bubbly.

Ginger Mint Relish

From An Herbal Affair In Your Kitchen!

Betty Breisch   1 ½ cups

1 cup fresh mint leaves
1 ½ cups raisins
2 tablespoons ground ginger
¼ cup sweet pickle relish
1 teaspoon shredded orange peel
½ teaspoon fresh lemon juice

- Grind mint leaves, raisins and ginger together. Stir in pickle relish, orange peel and lemon juice. Chill several hours before serving. Wonderful with cold lamb or turkey! Also excellent as topping on cream cheese for an appetizer.

Hint: May be stored 6 weeks in the refrigerator.

Green Chile Salsa

Ted Wheaton   2 cups

2 teaspoons olive oil
1 medium onion, coarsely chopped
2 large garlic cloves, minced
½ jalapeño pepper (optional)
1 can (14 ½ ounce) tomatoes with green chiles
1 teaspoon cumin
1 ½ teaspoon oregano
salt and pepper to taste

- Drain and chop tomatoes, reserving juice. Seed, devein and finely chop the jalapeño pepper.

- In a large skillet, heat the oil to medium. Add the onion, garlic and jalapeño. Cook until soft but not brown.

- Add tomatoes and chiles and simmer for 20 to 30 minutes over low heat, adding juice from the drained tomatoes if the sauce seems too dry. Remove from heat.

- Pulverize the cumin and oregano with mortar and pestle and add with other seasonings. Blend, cover and allow to cool in skillet.

Hint: Serve with eggs, grilled or roasted meats, beans, or tacos.

Pesto Sauce
From my childhood!

Pat Hosty   1 cup

3 cups fresh basil leaves, loosely packed
¾ cup olive oil
3 garlic cloves (or more)
¼ cup pine nuts
1 teaspoon salt
⅔ cup Parmesan cheese, grated

Pat said, "When I was a little girl, the housewives in my hometown in Illinois made this recipe using a mortar and pestle. In their long black dresses, they would grind away on these very same ingredients. Now we're blessed with our food processors to do the work and I don't wear long black dresses."

- Place all ingredients, except the Parmesan cheese, in a food processor. When smooth, pour sauce into a small bowl.
- Add Parmesan cheese and mix well. Taste and adjust the seasonings. Black or red pepper may be added to taste.
- Toss with hot cooked pasta, add to cold pasta salads, use as garnish for minestrone soup, or just spread on good old fashioned bread.
- Pesto may be frozen, but add the cheese after the sauce has thawed.

Candied Dill Chunks
A Symphony Showhouse Tea Room favorite!

Cynthia Hayes   4 cups

1 quart dill pickles, drained
½ cup tarragon vinegar
2 ¾ cups sugar
7 garlic cloves, peeled
2 tablespoons pickling spices
¼ teaspoon red pepper flakes, optional

- Mix vinegar, sugar and garlic cloves. Let stand about 4 hours, stirring at intervals until sugar dissolves.
- Place ½ of the pickles in jar and add spices tied in cheesecloth.
- Add remaining pickles and fill jar with syrup mixture. Cover. Refrigerate for 1 week before serving. Remove spices to serve. This keeps for several weeks in the refrigerator.

Minute Mayonnaise

Cecile Harrison   1 ½ cups

1 whole egg
2 tablespoons lemon juice
½ teaspoon dry mustard
½ teaspoon salt
dash of cayenne pepper
¾ cup vegetable oil
¼ cup olive oil

- Into a blender place egg, lemon juice, and seasonings. Add ¼ cup oil, cover and run 5 seconds.
- Remove cover, start blender, and gradually add the balance of the oil, stopping from time to time to let the mixture blend without additions. When all the oil has been added, run the blender for another 5 seconds.

Hint: With the addition of ¼ teaspoon garlic powder, this mayonnaise becomes the traditional French sauce for fish known as aioli.

White House Restaurant Dressing

Aileen Frank   1 pint

1 tablespoons flour
2 tablespoons sugar
1 teaspoon salt
1 teaspoon dry mustard
¼ cup white vinegar
¼ cup water
2 whole eggs, beaten
1 carton (8 ounce) thick sour cream

- Mix dry ingredients, add liquids and cook until thickened. Mix in the beaten eggs, whisking, over VERY low heat until thickened.
- Cool and stir in the sour cream.
- This is delicious served with artichokes, asparagus, and even on sandwiches.

The beautiful and gracious White House Restaurant is recalled with fond food memories.

Raspberry Vinegar

From the Sand Springs Herbal Festival!

Teresa Whitehead

1 ½ pints

**1 package (10 ounces) frozen
raspberries
3 cups vinegar
1 cup sugar**

• Strain berries and measure ¾ cup juice. Heat juice, vinegar and sugar to boiling, stirring frequently. Boil and stir one minute. Cool. Pour into bottles and cover tightly. Use in salad dressings, as marinade for steaks or on fresh vegetables.

Hint: Keep this in mind for a pretty Christmas gift. You may put berries in the bottle to make it decorative, or put berries on skewers in the bottle for another look. Blackberries may be substituted. Excellent!

Thousand Island Dressing

Symphony Showhouse Tea Room

60 servings

**1 cup chili sauce
2 quarts mayonnaise
4 teaspoons onions, minced
½ teaspoon Worcestershire sauce
6 eggs, hard cooked, chopped fine
1 cup sweet pickles, finely
chopped
2 teaspoons salt**

• Stir chili sauce into mayonnaise. Add onions, Worcestershire sauce, eggs, pickles and salt. Mix together thoroughly and chill.

Weepless Meringue Pie Topping 🖤

*Reprinted from **The Daily Oklahoman**.*

Norma Howe   Yield: Meringue for 1 pie

1 ½ teaspoon unflavored gelatin
1 tablespoon cornstarch
2 tablespoons cold water
½ cup boiling water
⅓ cup sugar
3 egg whites
¼ teaspoon cream of tartar
1 teaspoon vanilla extract

- Mix gelatin, cornstarch and water in a small saucepan. Stir until dissolved. Add boiling water; bring mixture to a boil and cook 1 minute, stirring constantly.

- Remove from heat and stir in sugar. Refrigerate exactly 25 minutes.

- Meanwhile, beat egg whites and cream of tartar until soft peaks form. Add the gelatin mixture (at 25 minutes!) and vanilla and continue beating until mixture is very stiff.

- Fill a 9 ½-inch baked crust with your favorite pie filling and top with meringue, being sure to seal by spreading meringue to all edges of the crust.

- Bake at 350 degrees (15 to 20 minutes) until lightly browned.

- May be kept covered in refrigerator after it's cool.

Pecan Sage Dressing

Thelma V. Jordan   6 servings

1 pound loaf stale white bread,
processed to crumbs
1 ½ cups onion, chopped
2 cups celery, chopped
½ cup butter, melted
½ cup pecans, ground
½ teaspoon salt
¼ teaspoon black pepper
¼ teaspoon rubbed sage
1 egg, well beaten
2 ¼ cups hot chicken or turkey
broth

- Preheat oven to 325 degrees.
- Sauté onion and celery in butter until tender. Place in a large bowl. Add crumbs and remaining ingredients. Toss well. Lightly spoon into a well-greased 8x8x2-inch baking dish. Bake for 40 to 45 minutes.

Taco Seasoning Mix

Marion DeVore   3 tablespoons

1 tablespoon chili powder
2 teaspoons onion powder
1 teaspoon ground cumin
1 teaspoon garlic powder
1 teaspoon paprika
1 teaspoon ground oregano
1 teaspoon sugar
½ teaspoon lite salt

- Mix all ingredients together in a small bowl and use as any purchased taco seasoning mix. The yield of this recipe is equal in strength to a 14 ounce package of commercial taco seasoning.

Sinful Hot Fudge Sauce

A Symphony Showhouse Tea Room favorite!

Dixie Gordon   Yield: 2 cups

4 squares (2 ounce) unsweetened
chocolate
½ cup butter
3 cups confectioner's sugar
1 ½ cups evaporated milk
1 teaspoon vanilla extract

- Melt chocolate and butter in a 4-quart pan over very low heat. Remove from heat. Turn burner up to medium.
- Add sugar alternately with milk, blending well with a wire whisk.
- Return the mixture to medium heat, bring to a boil, stirring constantly with the whisk for about 8 minutes. The Fudge Sauce will be thick and creamy. Stir in vanilla extract.

Hint: Store in a covered container in the refrigerator. Sauce may be reheated and thinned with evaporated milk, if necessary.

Lekvar

For the Festival of Purim!

Debbie Bloustine   Yield: 1 ½ cups

1 pound sweet prunes
3 orange slices, thinly cut
½ cup walnuts, ground
½ lemon, rind and juice
¼ cup sugar
1 tablespoon vegetable oil
dash of nutmeg

- Cook the prunes and the orange slices in a small amount of water until tender and the water has evaporated.
- Stone the cooked prunes and purée them with the remaining ingredients.
- Use this filling for Hamentaschen.

MIX AND MATCH MENU PLANNER

	Appetizer	Main Dish	Vegetables	Salads	Dessert
New Year's Dinner	Tortilla Soup Nutty Baked Camembert Champagne Punch	Baked Ham Pheasant Normandie Orange Roughey Louie	Squash Soufflé Perky Blackeyed Peas Fresh Steamed Broccoli	Cranberry Salad Blackeyed Pea Salad Calico Corn Salad	Bourbon Sweet Potato Pie Prohibition Whiskey Cake Chocolate Truffles
Valentine's Day	Bleu Crab Fondue Strawberry Lemonade Punch Cashew Chicken Balls	Chicken with Lime Butter Coquilles St. Jacque El Dorado Casserole	Wild Rice Bake Baked Potatoes Mixed Bean Casserole	Zucchini and Basil Salad Eggplant Pyramid Spinach Cups	Philbrook's Italian Cream Cake Coconut Mousse Strawberries Newport
Easter	Brie Soup Crab Stuffed Mushroom Caps Salmon Mousse	Mannheim Pork Roast Leg of Lamb Chicken Puttanesca	Asparagus Vinaigrette Baked Onions	Caesar Salad Frozen Fruit and Nut Medley	Bride's Bread Pudding Hammett House Lemon Pecan Pie
July 4th	Rum Mint Cooler Citrus Bourbon Slush Greek Cheese	Veal Paprika Enrico's Salmon Pork Chop with Apples	Broccoli on the Cool Side Snappy Spaghetti Squash	Ginger Ale Salad Assorted Greens with Raspberry Vinaigrette	Lemon Crumb Squares Fresh Strawberry Pie Elegant Daiquiri Soufflé
Labor Day	Frozen Margaritas Party Cheese Log Red Pepper Hors d'Oeuvres	Cheesy Onion Burger Buns with Burgers Smothers Swordfish Grilled Rack of Lamb	Chase Farm Cheese Grits Fresh Corn on the Cob Creamy Herbed Pasta	Molded Ambrosia Tossed Mixed Lettuces with White House Dressing	Pretty Boy's Apple Pie Peach Cobbler Chocolate on Chocolate Cheese Cake
Columbus Day	Chicken Liver Paté Sopa de Helote Okie Caviar	Herbed Pork Tenderloin Grilled Shrimp Beef Burgundy	Perle's Potato Salad Fresh Tomato Pasta	Cauliflower Salad Tossed Green Salad	Black Satin Fudge Cake Coffee Angel Food Cake Mighty Mousse
Thanksgiving	Hot Spiced Cider Cream of Pumpkin Soup Caviar Spread	Wild Goose Sherried Quail Traditional Roast Turkey	Baked Wild Rice Three Pea Medley Green Beans with Almonds	Amish Cole Slaw Frozen Fruit and Nut Medley Cranberry Grape Salad	Fruit Yogurt Pie Sour Cream Pecan Pie Pumpkin Ice Cream Pie
Christmas	Champagne Punch Hot Lobster Dip Turkey Green Chile Soup	Veal Paprika Roast Tenderloin Pork Forestiori	Candied Yam Boats Sour Cream Rice Pasta Primavera Vegetable Melange	Cranberry Grape Salad Jazzy Zucchini Salad Spinach Salad	Cream Puffs Pumpkin Pecan Pie Bananas Foster Pie
Birthday Party	Frozen Margaritas Teriyaki Chicken Wings Caponata	Boots Brats Karen's Burgers Raspberry Chicken Salad	Corn Casserole Potato Latkes Sauerkraut Supreme	Fresh Sliced Tomatoes Cucumbers and Onions	Birthday Cake with Vanilla Ice Cream and Sinful Hot Fudge Sauce French Meringue Cake Chocolate Bundt Cake
Bridge Luncheon	Rum Mint Cooler Yogurt Dip Crusty Seed Sticks	Ham-Spinach Torte Crab Cakes Orbach Frosted Chicken Salad	Wild Rice Pecan Pilaf Skillet Cabbage	Herbed Green Pea Salad Assorted Fresh Fruit	Shortbread Cookies Elegant Daiquiri Soufflé Baked Pear Elegance
Tail Gate Party or Outdoor Picnic	Grilled Lemon Butter Chicken Wings Ham Squares Rosemary Walnuts	Chicken Pie Chilean Style Barbeque Brisket Muffaletta Sandwiches	Red Rice and Beans Wewoka Baked Beans	Sliced cucumbers, tomatoes, onions and green peppers	Dvorsky's Dirt Mincemeat Filled Cookies Baked Fudge

COMMITTEE

Preliminary Research and Development

Adeanya Hunt	Tish Eason
Jill Mizel	Ellie Scherlag
Mona Preuss	Aileen Frank
JoAnn Arneson	Dixie Gordon
Marge Duncan	Ava Wheaton
Jeanne Blair	Priscilla Braun
Joe Hunt	Jane Coalson
Berta Faye Rex	

Recipe Chairmen
Oklahoma City Orchestra League

Kay Lindsey	Jean Fishburne

Oklahoma Festival Fare

Colleen Green	June Rickey

Celebrity Specialties

Alan Valentine	Eddie Walker

Testing and Selection Chairmen

Pam Woolbright	Carole Almond
Donita Phillips	Carol Sue Taylor

Nutrition Analysis

Jean Hartsuck, Ph.D.

Editorial Staff

Colleen Blaylock Green
Pat Taliaferro
Pam Woolbright
Mary Jo Nelson, Consultant

Proof Readers

Pat Taliaferro	JoAnn Arneson
Garline Wheatley	Cissy Long
Ann Taylor	Ava Wheaton

Computer Staff

Debbie Ritter	Pat Taliaferro
Garline Wheatley	Nancy Apgar
Colleen Green	June Rickey
Marilyn Ehlers, Consultant	

Graphic Design Director

Linda Garrett

APPLAUSE Artist

Virginia Vann

Photography

Roger Short

Marketing Development and Sales Research

Pat Hosty
Joanne Harrah
Kay Floyd
William Pirtle, Consultant

COOKBOOK PROJECT DIRECTOR

Nancy S. Apgar

APPLAUSE

Sincere appreciation is extended to each of the following people who played such an important role in raising the curtain on **Applause**, Oklahoma's Best Performing Recipes. Additionally, each and every member of the Oklahoma City Orchestra League, over 400 strong, who believed in the cookbook project and worked to make it all possible, deserve many curtain calls.

In several instances, the same or a very similar recipe was submitted by more than one contributor. The committee has made every attempt, from over 3000 recipes, to truly bring to you Oklahoma's **Best** Performing Recipes. If anyone has been inadvertently omitted from this list, we apologize.

Brava to each and everyone who played a part.

Steve Allen
Carole Almond
Murdeen Anderson
Nancy Apgar
Paula Apgar
JoAnn Arneson
Michael Ashcraft
Jeannette Atwood
Jane Baker
Malea L. Barber
Catherine Mae Bardwell
Louise Barnes
Manuel Barrueco
Louise Barry
Gay Bartley
Katie Bates
John Bennett
Esther Bernstein
Louise Berry
Freida Biddle
Vince Bishop
Jeannie Blair
Debbie Bloustine
Pat Bond
Steve Bond
Grace Boulton
Pat Bowlan
Jan Bowles
Glenna Boyd
Delores Boyle
Nellie Brandell
Karyn Brandt
Mary Braum
Priscilla Braun
Kathleen Howe Bressie
Betty Breisch
Libby Britton
Becky Buchanan
Pat Buchanan
Lois Jean Buck
Gretta Burnett
Betty Burnham
Mary Beebe Butts
Sandi Byerly
Jeanne Byler
Walta Carmichael
Neal Carrick
Karen Casabon
Virgie Casselman
Beverly Gale Chadwell

Linda Coats
Georgia Collins
Judy Collins
Wanda Cook
Beverly Coon
Kathryn Cooper
Mattie Lee Cory
Eloise Cost
Barbara Crabtree
Myles Criss
Steve Daniels
Helen Danner
Carol David
Bella Davidovich
Chip Davis
Karen Davis
Marion De Vore
Nancy DeCordova
Mischa Dichter
Ruth Dick
Patricia Dickey
Dorothy Dinsmoor
Reta Dohrer
Alice Dotter
Barry Douglas
Sharon Dow
Dee Downard
Jeannie Drake
Dee Dugan
Debra Duncan
Doris Duncan
Marge Duncan
George Dvorsky
Tish Easton
Neta Ebert
Margaret Eckroat
Virginia Edwards
Kristy Ehlers
Marilyn Ehlers
Dee Ann Ellis
Dolores Elms
Betty Elton
Helen S. Fay
Martha Lou Findeiss
Ethel Findlay
Jean Fishburne
Yvette Fleckinger
Sandra Flesher
Betty K. Fletcher
Kay Floyd

Mary Fors
Aileen Frank
John Frank
Mary Frates
Mex Frates
Carol Frazee
Russ Frazee
Señora Luis Herrera
Peggy Gandy
Garden Restaurant
Susan J. Garner
Lu Garrison
Maurine Gatewood
Joan Gilmore
Nancy Gomez
Dorris Goodbary
Betty Gordon
Dixie Gordon
Scott Gordon
Gary Graffman
Colleen Blaylock Green
Cinderella Groce
Helen Grove
Pennie Hain
Minna Hall
Almeda Hamilton
Hammett House Restaurant
Patty Hampton
Jane Harlow
Joanne Harrah
EmmyLou Harris
Cecile Harrison
Jack Harrold
Valerie Kerr Hart
Jean Hartsuck
Dorothy Hassler
Mary Hassler
Susan Hatcher
Cynthia Hayes
Carey Head
Diane Henderson
Pat Higgins
Frank J. Hightower
Eleanor Hill
Sharon Hodder
Billie Hodgell
Nadine Holloway
Celeste Holm
Sue Hood
Patricia K. Hosty

Norma Howe
Adeanya Hunt
Ann Hunt
Joe Hunt
Julia Hunt
Priscilla Hunt
Evelyn Janeway
Jane Jayroe
Dixie Jensen
Benita Johnson
Betty Johnson
Dora Mae Jones
Jackie Jones
Thelma V. Jordan
Bill Kamp
Betty Schmahl Kay
Lynn Kelly
Leona Kemp
Tom Kemper
Fran Kennemer
Lou Kerr
Robert S. Kerr, Jr.
Shari Kerr
Lynn Kickingbird
Martha King
Mary King
Nancy King
Russell King
Julia Kirkpatrick
Lucille Kirschner
Jeannie Klaassen
Amy Kerson Kohn
Berniece Kostboth
Robin Leach
Carolyn Leake
Lorraine Lear
Ida Mae Lehman
Diann Lemons
Joel Levine
Elaine Levy
Laura Lewis
Mitzie Lilly
Kay Lindsey
Cissy Long
Clella Lookabaugh
Jerry Love
Kathryn Lowry
Afaf Mahfouz
Ina Lou Marquis
Juanita Martin
Fred Marvel
Sue Massey
Karen Mayfield
McAlester's Italian Festival
Penny McCaleb
Marilyn McCoo
Barbara McCune
Rachel McGee
Maureen McGovern
Nancy McGuire
Peg McGwire
Sally McKee
Jody McLane
Mennonite Community of Corn
Mennonite Community of
Fairview
Barbara Merrill
Barbara Messenbaugh
Nancy Midkiff
Donna Miller

Verna Miller
Carol Cole Mills
Jill Mizel
Jenny Montgomery
Pauline Morgan
Pexim (Phaik-Sim) Mui
Phyllis Murray
Jim Nabors
Joyce Neathery
Mary Jo Nelson
Yvonne Nichols
Marilyn North
Linda Vann Odom
Laura Kerr Ogle
Oklahoma Dept. of Tourism
Bob Olson
Phyllis Olson
Sara Olson
Harriette G. Orbach
Leroy Orsborn
Thelma Ortner
Mabel L. Osborne
Elliott Oshay
Loretta O'Hara
June Parry
Angela Patrone
Marilyn Paul
Glenda Payne
Itzhak Perlman
Mattie Perryman
Barbara Peters
Christine Peters
Frieda Peters
Jean Petito
Donita Phillips
Loretta Pickhardt
Lou Pinkerton
Judy Pirtle
Barbara Pool
Mona Preuss
Betty Price
Laura Pritchard
Robbie Quillan
Rosemary Ragland
Ruth Ralston
Florence N. Ratzlaff
Berta Faye Rex
June Rickey
Debbie Ritter
Bobbi Robbins
Carol Robertson
Frances Robinson
Susan Robinson
Gertrude Rodman
Lil Ross
Carol Rowland
Edward Russell
Jo Russell
Grace Ryan
Patsy Sallee
Carolyn Sandusky
Avis Scaramucci
Ellie Scherlag
Caroline Schieren
Ina Mae Schlegel
Bob Schmidt
Wanda Sellers
George Seminoff
Lou Shepherd
JoRene Sherburne

Sylvia Shirley
Glenn Shoaf
Dennis Shrock
Beth Shumway
Jeannette Sias
Ann Simms
Patsy Sinclair
Anne Skinner
Carol Smaglinski
Betty Smith
Smothers Brothers
Jeannine F. Spencer
Jacquelyn Stengel
Kay Stevens
Feodora Steward
Cynthia Williams Stewart
Phyllis Stough
Olga Streich
Mary Stuart
Millicent Sukman
Libby Sullivan
Mary Helen Swanson
Mary Gordon Taft
Boots Taliaferro
Pat Taliaferro
Ann Taylor
Carol Sue Taylor
Fra Taylor
Pat Thomas
Shauna Thomas
Trish Thomas
Sue Timberlake
Joanna Todd
Tishomingo, Chickasaw Festval
Linda Trippe
Barbara Tunell
Alan Valentine
Kay Valentine
James Vallion
Virginia Vann
Susan Wadley
Eddie Walker
Michael Wallis
Jody Walls
Orene Walters
David Ward
Marcia Ward
Eve Wegener
Sidney Weiss
Garline Johnson Wheatley
Ava Wheaton
Theodore Wheaton
Betsy White
Theresa Whitehead
Nancy Whittier
Georgiana Wiesner
Barbara Bonifazi Williams
Carol Williams
Nettie Williams
Rosalee Williams
Sandra Williams
Amy Winineger
Fran Wise
Patty Withrow
Nancy Witter
Jan Woodson
Pam Frazee Woolbright
Stan Zerbst

251

APPLAUSE

Applause
Oklahoma City Orchestra League, Inc.
Fifty Penn Place, R-325
Oklahoma City, OK 73118

Order Form

Send ____ copies of Applause at $17.95 per copy plus postage and handling ($2.50 per book).

Enclosed is check for $_____. In Oklahoma, add sales tax.

Charge my Visa or Mastercard No. _____ Exp. date_____

Signature _____

Name (print) _____

Address_____

City_____State_____Zip_____

Applause
Oklahoma City Orchestra League, Inc.
Fifty Penn Place, R-325
Oklahoma City, OK 73118

Order Form

Send ____ copies of Applause at $17.95 per copy plus postage and handling ($2.50 per book).

Enclosed is check for $_____. In Oklahoma, add sales tax.

Charge my Visa or Mastercard No. _____ Exp. date_____

Signature _____

Name (print) _____

Address_____

City_____State_____Zip_____

Applause
Oklahoma City Orchestra League, Inc.
Fifty Penn Place, Suite R-325
Oklahoma City, OK 73118

Gift Order

Send ____ copies of Applause at $17.95 per copy plus postage and handling ($2.50 per book).

Enclosed is check for $_____. In Oklahoma, add sales tax.   ☐Gift Wrap, $1.00 each.

Charge my Visa or Mastercard No. _____ Exp. date_____

Signature _____

To: (Name)_____

Address_____

City_____State_____Zip_____

From: (Name)_____

Address_____

City_____State_____Zip_____

RE-ORDER ADDITIONAL COPIES

Names and addresses of bookstores, gift shops, etc. in your area would be appreciated.

_____

_____

_____

_____

_____

Names and addresses of bookstores, gift shops, etc. in your area would be appreciated.

_____

_____

_____

_____

_____

Names and addresses of bookstores, gift shops, etc. in your area would be appreciated.

_____

_____

_____

_____

_____